Confident UX

Confident UX

*The essential skills for
user experience design*

Adrian Bilan

KoganPage

Publisher's note
Every possible effort has been made to ensure that the information contained in this book is accurate at the time of going to press, and the publishers and authors cannot accept responsibility for any errors or omissions, however caused. No responsibility for loss or damage occasioned to any person acting, or refraining from action, as a result of the material in this publication can be accepted by the editor, the publisher or the author.

First published in Great Britain and the United States in 2023 by Kogan Page Limited

2nd Floor, 45 Gee Street
London
EC1V 3RS
United Kingdom

8 W 38th Street, Suite 902
New York, NY 10018
USA

4737/23 Ansari Road
Daryaganj
New Delhi 110002
India

www.koganpage.com

Kogan Page books are printed on paper from sustainable forests.

© Kogan Page 2023

ISBNs

Hardback	978 1 3986 1303 4
Paperback	978 1 3986 1301 0
Ebook	978 1 3986 1302 7

British Library Cataloguing-in-Publication Data

A CIP record for this book is available from the British Library.

Library of Congress Cataloging-in-Publication Data
2023942803

Typeset by Integra Software Services, Pondicherry
Print production managed by Jellyfish
Printed and bound by CPI Group (UK) Ltd, Croydon, CR0 4YY

To my grandmother
for teaching me what's possible

To my twins
for defying the impossible

To my wife
for making it all possible

Contents

List of figures and tables

Acknowledgements

Reading a book changes the way you see the world. I knew that. I've experienced it so many times before. What I didn't know was that when you are the one writing the book, you get to change the world.

Writing this, I've also realized, in some ways, that a book is the sum of your life experiences. It's all the people that shaped your destiny, all your dreams, all the mistakes you've made and the lessons you've learned. I've discovered that when you write, you reconnect with your past. So, this is me saying thank you to everyone who was there for me along the way.

First, I would like to thank my family, particularly my wife, Alina, who always inspired and supported me. Without you, I wouldn't be the person I am today. I would like to thank my twins, George and Jack, for all the happiness they bring into my life. I am so proud of you two! Thank you to my grandmother Aurelia and my grandfather Gheorghe for teaching me to be kind, no matter what. I miss you both so much! Thank you to my mother, Dana, for always believing in me and to my father, Dragos, for introducing me to the world of technology, a path that I would end up following to this day. Thank you to my brother, Stefan, who showed me you can overcome any obstacle. Thank you to my mother-in-law, Mariana, for all her hard work and dedication to our family. Thank you to my father-in-law, Aurel, for all the interesting stories he shared and to my brother-in-law, Victor, for all the entertaining moments we spent together.

Thank you, Daniel Marina, for years and years of debates about technology, design and human nature. Thank you Nick Read for our conversations around product management, UX and life in general. Thank you to all my teachers and mentors and in particular Andrea Picchi, for inspiring me (maybe without knowing) to write my own book. Thank you Ersan Hakki for all the wisdom you shared with me all these years. Thank you to all my colleagues at CBRE – I've learned so much from each and every one of you. A big thank you to Tom Scott, who's influenced my career in more ways than he can imagine.

You wouldn't be reading any of this if not for the incredibly talented team at Kogan Page. First, I want to thank my commissioning editor Matt James for believing in me and for all the support during this entire process. Thank you to my copy-editor, Alison Elks, for making sure this book is well-written. Finally, I would like to thank the marketing team, Jaini Haria and Bruna Sperotto, for guiding me through all their efforts. Also, a big thank you to everyone else who was involved in the design, editing, printing and publishing.

Finally, I would like to thank you, the one reading this book, for taking an interest in the amazing field of UX. I can promise you one thing: it will never cease to amaze you!

Introduction

Welcome to the world of user experience (UX) design. If you're reading this, it's likely you're an aspiring designer, developer, product manager, or perhaps a business stakeholder or entrepreneur looking to improve how people interact with their product or service. Or you're just curious about how to create products that people *actually want to use*. Whatever your background, you're in the right place.

In this book we'll dive into UX design's nitty-gritty, from understanding and capturing user needs, creating user personas or wireframes, to designing user interfaces and prototypes, conducting usability testing and confidently presenting to your stakeholders. We'll also explore some of the latest UX design methods and how to apply them to your products. But don't worry, I'll keep it light and simple because, let's be honest, reading a technical book can sometimes be about as exciting as watching paint dry (unless you're into that kind of thing, in which case, I won't judge).

In all seriousness, UX design is essential for creating successful products and services. It's about understanding the needs and wants of the people using a product; and designing a solution that not only meets those needs but aims to exceed them. It's about creating a seamless and enjoyable experience for the user that they'll want to return to again and again.

Think of it this way: imagine walking into a store to buy a new pair of sunglasses. The store is cluttered and disorganized, the glasses are all jumbled together and the salesperson is nowhere to be found. Frustrating, right? Now imagine walking into a store where the sunglasses are neatly arranged by size and style, the salesperson is friendly and helpful and the whole experience is enjoyable. Which store are you more likely to return to? That right there is the power of UX. And it's not just about making something look pretty. It's about creating a positive and satisfying experience for the user. In this book, we'll explore how to do that, from A to Z.

PART ONE

What is UX design?

Today's technology has enabled businesses to create innovative solutions that provide faster delivery times, access to global markets and improved product quality.

As a result, companies are investing heavily in research and development to stay ahead of their competition by leveraging new technologies such as artificial intelligence (AI), machine learning (ML), blockchain, augmented reality (AR), virtual reality (VR), etc. These technologies have opened up new horizons and helped improve customer engagement, increase sales conversions, reduce costs associated with the production and distribution of goods or services, enhance security for better data protection and much more.

However, all this would not be possible without considering user experience. The birth of this new world of possibilities has changed the way we interact with products and services. The appetite for a great user experience is increasing as customers now expect more from the products or services they purchase – these now need to be tailored to meet their specific needs, and this is non-negotiable. The bar has been raised!

If you're wondering how UX design might help you be better positioned in a rapidly changing business world, in Part One we'll take a journey through the basic elements of UX design, from the definition and key components that make up successful products and services, all the way to future technologies and trends. Let's dive right in!

CHAPTER ONE

An introduction to user experience

A t its core, UX design is about understanding human behaviour and designing products around those behaviours in order to create enjoyable products or services for users.

UX designers take into account not only the functionality of a product but also its aesthetics – how it looks and feels to use – and all the emotions it conveys when interacted with. The goal is to create an enjoyable user experience that promotes a positive connection between the user and the product or service they're interacting with. This emotional connection helps us build trust, loyalty and engagement, which can ultimately lead to improved business outcomes.

As UX designers, we must remember that emotions play an essential role in driving user behaviour and must be thoughtfully considered when researching and designing products or services. Therefore, understanding emotion-driven design principles is something any aspiring UX designer who wants to create successful user experiences should do. Luckily, I will show you how to do just that in the section 'Human experience'.

History does not repeat itself, but it rhymes

Before I start going into more detail about what UX is, I think it would be helpful for you to understand a bit of the history that contributed to user experience as a discipline. So here we go.

The history of UX

'It's a tale as old as time,' some say, or at least 'as old as the digital age,' others say. They are all probably right, but I'll get to that in a bit.

Once upon a time, in the glory days of the early internet, when UX wasn't even an afterthought, websites were clunky, confusing and about as user-friendly as a cactus. Have any of you ever seen those fonts or animated gifs from the early internet? A sight to be seen.

As the internet evolved and more people got online, companies began to realize that treating users like human beings (instead of just hit counter stats) could be good for business (I know, right?). It was 1993 when Don Norman, a cognitive psychologist and designer who at the time was working for Apple, coined the term 'user experience'.[1] Thus, the field of UX was officially born. Later, together with Jakob Nielsen, Don Norman went ahead and built Nielsen Norman Group (NN/g), one of the most prestigious UX organizations in the world, and UX became a discipline that today is indispensable for the success of any product.

But did UX actually start there? Is it truly 'as old as the digital age'? I think not. UX is a multidisciplinary field; and it draws its principles from disciplines and human innovations that happened over time. Let's think about it for a moment. What other disciplines or events have contributed to UX becoming what it is today? When I reflect on this I always remember Steve Jobs' 2005 Stanford commencement address (I encourage you to watch the whole video); his words 'You can't connect the dots looking forward; you can only connect them looking backwards' make so much sense.[2] This is certainly true for both UX as a discipline but also your own future career in this amazing field (and you will see why in Chapter 13). So, let's do just that – let's try to connect the dots moving backwards.

UX as a field has deep roots in human factors and ergonomics, a domain that also uses multiple other sub-disciplines to understand human behaviour and apply that knowledge to the design and creation of products and services. This, for example, is one of many official definitions, according to *The Dictionary for Human Factors/Ergonomics* by James H. Stramler:

> Human factors is that field which is involved in conducting research regarding human psychological, social, physical, and biological characteristics, maintaining the information obtained from that research, and working to apply that information with respect to the design, operation, or use of products or systems for optimizing human performance, health, safety, and/or habitability.[3]

How does it feel reading that? Isn't it very close to what UX is today for both digital and physical products? But how can that be? They are still different fields, aren't they? This is where it gets interesting. UX design draws its strength from so many other domains. The very fabric of design relies on multidisciplinarity, and UX design is no exception to that. As a discipline, UX borrows from psychology, research, data science, industrial design, writing, architecture, human–computer interaction (HCI), sound and motion design, technology, visual design, etc. The list can go on and on, and it's growing each year with every new advancement in technology.

So many events have influenced what UX is today that trying to understand which one had the most impact is an impossible task. UX is an organically self-built discipline, and that is the sheer beauty of it. There are so many things that come to mind that might have aided the formation of UX, like Henry Dreyfuss's book *Designing for People*[4] – where we see the first clear signs of choosing to include people and their bespoke needs in the rationale behind design decisions or the Toyota production system that created a giant leap forward in terms of management systems and later organically influenced software engineering and digital product design as we know them today, or perhaps the many advancements in cognitive science that were made in the 1960s. And these are just some of the examples. We could probably find many, many more. What I'm trying to say is that no matter what field you're coming from it is very likely that it's connected to UX in some shape or form, and later in this book I'll show you why it's essential to capitalize on that.

Now let's go back to the early days of the internet (1990s to 2000). It was a slow start, but websites started to look less like a carnival of chaos and more like a carefully curated collection of actual digestible content. Navigation became more friendly, layouts became more intuitive, and the dreaded '404 error' page was replaced with a more jovial 'Oops, this page can't be found'. Those were the times! Luckily good design, at its core is done through iterations and continuous improvement, so the tech landscape at the time was the environment where UX could thrive and find itself as a discipline.

It's been a wild ride ever since, with new technologies and design trends constantly emerging, but one thing definitely passed the test of time: understanding the user leads to happier customers and better products.

As UX design gained popularity, its definition and scope started to expand. Soon, it wasn't just about making websites usable, it was about *creating a holistic and seamless experience* across all touchpoints of a product or service. From websites and apps, to physical products and in-store experiences, UX design started to touch every aspect of business and technology. And it's not just about making things look pretty, it's about solving real problems and creating value for users.

As technology continues to advance at a rapid pace, the role of UX will only become more vital in creating products and services that are not only useful but also delightful to use. The history of UX is a story of change, where design and technology have evolved hand in hand to better serve the needs of people.

Not another boring definition...

I know that these books often begin with a list of boring definitions, but stay with me for a second! We've all heard the term 'UX' before, but what does it actually mean? It's easy to shrug off UX as just another buzzword, but in reality it is incredibly important to understand how UX is actually defined because this will later help you shape your career or the product you are working on. So, let's take a look at how UX is defined by the design industry and how it can be used to create unforgettable user experiences. We'll even go beyond this and explore the different elements that make up UX design, from user research and testing to visual design. By understanding these core concepts, you'll have a better appreciation of why UX matters so much in creating successful products.

To capture what UX is we need to understand what are the prerequisites for a great user experience. Let's look at what NN/g has to say on the matter:

> The first requirement for an exemplary user experience is to meet the exact needs of the customer, without fuss or bother. Next comes simplicity and elegance that produces products that are a joy to own, a joy to use. True user experience goes far beyond giving customers what they say they want, or providing checklist features. In order to achieve high-quality user experience in a company's offerings there must be a seamless merging of the services of multiple disciplines, including engineering, marketing, graphical and industrial design, and interface design.

It's important to distinguish the total user experience from the user interface (UI), even though the UI is obviously an extremely important part of the design. As an example, consider a website with movie reviews. Even if the UI for finding a film is perfect, the UX will be poor for a user who wants information about a small independent release if the underlying database only contains movies from the major studios.[5]

So what are the fundamental takeaways from this? I would like you to remember three key things from NN/g's description of UX that I will often reiterate in different forms throughout this book:

- The most important thing about UX is user-centricity. If you do not involve users, it's likely that you are *not* doing UX.
- User experience is not about giving the customer just a set of features they asked for, but rather looking at the entire experience holistically and making sure everything works together seamlessly. You own the vision!
- While UI might be part of UX, they are not interchangeable, and they cannot exist without each other. Without UX, UI is just decoration. More on this topic later in Chapter 7.

So, what is UX made of? What are the core components of UX? User experience as a discipline includes research, design, evaluation, strategy and vision:

- *Research:* This concerns understanding the users, their needs, and their goals through methods such as user interviews, surveys, and usability testing. It's also important to look at both quantitative data (analytics) and qualitative data (data resulting from interviews, i.e. usability testing). This sits at the very epicentre of UX. A more complete look at this is provided in Chapter 5.
- *Design:* This involves creating a design solution that addresses the user needs and goals we've captured through research.

This can include creating sketches, wireframes, prototypes, and user flows.

- *Evaluation:* You cannot aim to be a successful UXer without testing the design solutions with users to gather feedback and measure its effectiveness. This includes usability testing, A/B testing and other forms of user research.

- *UX strategy:* Often overlooked and underestimated, this is the art of effectively communicating, presenting your work and managing stakeholder expectations and reactions. As you can imagine, it's not as easy as it may sound (picture yourself in front of a confused C-suite when you're presenting the new design) – luckily, we'll talk more about this in Chapter 9, so you're covered.

- *Vision:* This is a future aspirational view of what the user experience will look like. Together with the product manager, the UX team is responsible for shaping this vision. Ok, why is this so important? Because a product without a vision is just a collection of features. It misses the most important strategic elements that make the difference between a successful product and a mediocre one.

Keep in mind that this is just a high-level overview of what UX is comprised of, and user experience can include many other additional components depending on the context. Confused? Here's an example: you are tasked to design the user experience for a next-generation AI chatbot. All of a sudden, the UI takes a back seat, and the phrase 'content is king' has a lot more meaning to you. You will now need to master content strategy and content generation techniques at a totally different level. It is likely that you will need to study some basic natural language processing (NLP), perhaps dip into conversational interfaces and spice it up with some potential large language models like OpenAI's GPT. See how the context can change everything? We never have a boring day in the world of UX.

I can promise you that by the end of this book your confidence levels will be entirely different. Yes, UX can be a very complex field. Yes, you will encounter situations where you will ask yourself, 'Can I actually do this? But, I don't have the skills.' All I'll say to that is – 'Don't give up; this is normal.' One thing about UX is it will constantly push you out of your comfort zone because of its multidisciplinary nature. You can't be expected to be an expert in all those fields, right? You will also most likely be part of a team and can count on the support of others. True, but UX has this funny thing about it – you will naturally get familiar with those sub-disciplines depending on your existing skills, the opportunities you'll have in your career and your future aspirations. To conclude: don't feel threatened by this complexity. It also comes with a beautiful logic behind it all – and eventually, one day you will master it and smile looking back.

What UX is *not*

We started with the definition of UX and also looked at some of the main components that bring it to life. However, you might still have some doubts about what user experience is, and that is pretty normal. It can take thousands of hours of study and practice to understand the full depths of this discipline. One thing that really helped me over time was to build my so-called 'That's *not* UX' list, which is essentially a collection of examples that illustrate the sometimes messy world of user experience.

I want to share some of these 'experiences' with you because we live in an imperfect world, and not everything that comes out bearing the signature 'made by UX' is actual UX. Although I would never wish that upon you, you will definitely encounter some of these in your own career. Try to remember them as fun learning challenges that can only strengthen you as a professional. So, let's dive in.

UX without the user is not UX

This one is the mother of all UX offences. It's no surprise that UX is important in today's digital world – it's the difference between a successful product and one that fails.

But here's the thing – sometimes stakeholders, or even worse UX designers, try to take a shortcut and skip the user research. *Bad idea!* UX without user research is like building a house without any blueprints – it's just not going to turn out well. Research helps UX designers understand their users' needs, wants and habits, and this will ultimately inform their design decisions and help create a superior product.

So, what should you do if you're in a situation where user research isn't possible? I say 'possible', because, very likely, some stakeholders will try to convince you to 'just design it, we'll do research later'. My advice is to take the time to evangelize why user research (UR) is so important and why there cannot be UX without UR. Make sure your stakeholders understand the value of having user research data and the return on investment of doing this work – it can be the difference between success or failure. Work to make it possible! I will go into more detail on how to effectively communicate with your stakeholders in Chapter 9.

Ultimately, UX without user research is a gamble – you might get it right, but it just means you got lucky, so as you can imagine, the chances are slim. And also, remember, 'Although the field of user experience has gained popularity, bad design practices still exist in many organizations'.[6] As a designer, one of your roles is to question existing processes and apply your knowledge to make sure that the best practices are being implemented.

UX with the wrong users is not UX

This is a variation of the previous scenario. In all honesty, I believe this one to be slightly worse. Doing UX with the wrong users is tantamount to UX doom. Let me explain why. While in the first scenario, the UX designer, product manager or stakeholder that made the decision did so consciously with an assumed risk and they might intend to do it properly at some point, in this second scenario, in most cases, they will think they have already done the right thing. They *did* the user research, so everything will work out just fine. Unfortunately, this is not the case. They'll be making decisions based on an inaccurate or misleading understanding of their users, and as UX design is all about creating value for the user this is a big UX no-no.

UX design is a crucial part of any product development process, and selecting the right users for UX research is paramount to getting it right. Unfortunately, in many cases, product teams make the mistake of choosing the wrong people to conduct user research with. A few good examples would be: using colleagues or friends instead of real users; using random people outside the target audience because 'they're still users'; or, even worse, using proxy users instead of the actual users of the product. By proxy users, I mean people like support centre staff, the marketing team, the sales team, consultants that are close to the client, etc. I don't believe their input is not valuable; on the contrary, they hold key information, but they can't completely replace your actual user. By all means capture their thoughts, but don't forget your real user.

Choosing the wrong users can lead to disastrous results and expose the product to significant risks. It could mean that vital insights are missed, experiences become skewed, and the final product doesn't meet customer needs.

This might seem like UX 101, but unfortunately there are still UX designers who miss this step in their process and end up designing a product that fails. So if you find yourself in this situation or know someone who is taking shortcuts with UX research, here's the advice they need: *Don't do it!*

UX done in isolation is not UX

You've done your research, spent quality time with users and analysed all that data. You know have everything you need to create the perfect design. Users will love it, and the product will be a massive success. Do just this, and – it will probably fail.

'Wait, what?' you will ask. 'I've done all the hard work, I've created an amazing design and user experience.' Well, not really. Not if you've done it in isolation, enclosed in your UX ivory tower.

UX doesn't work in a vacuum. UX is part of a larger picture, including stakeholders, product managers and engineers, all making sure the design is feasible and aligns with the business strategy. If, as UX designers, you don't involve them in the UX process, you risk creating designs that are great on paper, perhaps great when tested with users, but don't work in reality. Confused? Let me explain. Without validating whether a product is viable and feasible, all you're doing is ending up with great ideas that don't work in practice. And nobody likes wasted effort! Imagine you do your research, create an amazing design, test it with users – who are all happy but fail to understand business goals or feasibility. Will this benefit the business? Is it sustainable for the business? Can this be technically done within a reasonable timeline and within budget? Do we have the skills and knowledge to do it? As a UX designer, you need to make sure you ask all these questions.

So, if you are a designer and find yourself in a UX process without stakeholders, product managers or engineers involved, take it as a sign to stop. Try to include them and make sure they have an active role in the UX design process. It will save time and money while creating better designs and happier users. That is UX done right!

UX too late is not UX

As UX designers, we sometimes fall in love with our craft. We study and put into practice the best methods for designing the most pleasing user experience. We interview users and involve stakeholders and engineers in the process. We structure and analyse all the data, coming up with conclusions, reports and recommendations. We then facilitate and run ideation workshops to put all that research to good use. We sketch, wireframe, prototype and test again with users... and then, we don't deliver on time! I know what you're going to say. 'Here we go again!' Trust me on this one; there is a tendency to become too purist in UX design, follow every single process by the book, do everything right and at the same time forget about the realities of the product and its business goals. *Don't try to boil the ocean.*

For those of you who are aspiring UX designers, if you ever run into this situation here's my advice: prioritize and time-box your UX efforts. Be aware of the product roadmap! Be aware of your delivery speed! Be aware of busy calendars and holidays! Create a UX roadmap that defines key milestones, so you can deliver user experiences just in time or, ideally, ahead of development sprints. And breathe! It's ok to compromise if it means getting the job done faster and meeting the deadlines.

Be pragmatic while also ensuring UX integrity; remember that, without delivery, UX work is just an academic exercise. That's why UX designers need to be aware of the commercial goals behind their designs, while continuously monitoring and optimizing the user experience. If done properly, UX design can help a product meet its goals without sacrificing user needs or the quality of UX – it just requires time-boxing initiatives and aligning UX processes with the realities of your product.

UX without the bigger picture is not UX

First, let me explain what I mean by the bigger picture. This will be particularly noticeable if you'll be working within a bigger, perhaps global, organization where there is an increased number of products, some of which are linked together by data or internal processes. They are all in different stages of a product life cycle – some are legacy, some are quite mature and some are freshly launched, while others are third-party off-the-shelves tools. A sight to be seen and quite the UX challenge. As designers, when we are faced with this situation, we have to step back and look at the entire environment – the bigger picture. What have we already built? Where did it come from? Are there any duplications or inconsistencies between different UX designs and user journeys? How does data flow from one system to another? In what sequence? etc. All these questions should be asked to ensure that we are taking into account all the other elements around us. UX designers must have an eagle eye for detail and a holistic mindset to really understand how everything fits together and flows. The secret is to be able to work at both levels at the same time.

My advice to you if you find yourselves in this situation is – dig deep! Do your research and make sure you understand what has been done before, so that you don't end up re-inventing the wheel or creating inconsistencies. Connect to the other UX designers or product managers in the team and share your knowledge – UX is a collaborative process after all! And finally, always keep an eye on how everything fits together and flows over time in the bigger picture – it will help you to build better UX.

Just UI is not UX

This one is a bit tricky, but it's an important distinction. I say tricky because UI is in fact part of UX as a discipline. As you already know by now, UX stands for user experience and is focused on understanding user needs and how they interact with digital products. UX can include activities such as user research, discovery workshops, ideation sessions and user testing – all of which are essential to a successful product. On the other hand, UI stands for user interface and is more about the visual elements of the design, such as layouts, colour palettes, typography, visual hierarchy, etc. It is the actual look and feel of the website or app that you create in your early sketches and prototypes.

Both put together, are a powerful tool. You know what you need to design, for whom and how. You've based your design choices on solid research, validated them with stakeholders and users and chosen the best interactions to satisfy the user requirements. But it doesn't always occur this way. Sometimes UI design is done in isolation, without user research, and without understanding what the target audience is or needs. This is sometimes done under pressure from inexperienced stakeholders or clients that want to save time or budget. Needless to say, this is the worst possible way of doing that.

No matter how good your UI looks and feels, if it's not based on actual user needs, the overall user experience will be a failure. People usually are more likely to forgive a less eye-catching and modern interface, but if you don't give them what they need they will never use it again.

If you're a UX designer who encounters a situation where UX isn't taken into account when designing a user interface, the best you can do is to try and encourage your colleagues or clients to understand the importance of doing UX to its full extent. First, educate them about UX and show them how research and ideation can help improve user experiences. Explain that UX is more than just UI – it's a *holistic approach* to considering all aspects of a user's experience with an interface or product, from usability to aesthetics. Explain the risks of doing just a pretty interface. Finally, always encourage people to test the UI with actual users, by building interactive prototypes. Show them how feedback can help identify potential problems or unexpected user needs early, before they arise in production – all this before you need to write even one line of code (and that does actually save budget). Lastly, don't be afraid to stand your ground – UX is a valuable part of the product development process and skipping it can be costly. It is your job to defend it. I will cover this topic in a bit more detail in Chapter 7.

Human experience

At its core, UX is indeed about users, and user experience is often thought of as more of a technical field, but in reality that's not entirely true. Yes, UX means designing and developing products (in many cases digital) such as websites or mobile apps that are easy to use and provide value to the user.

Call me sentimental, but there is much more to UX than meets the eye. There is this deep connection that goes beyond digital, or beyond the product you are working on. It goes beyond the processes, the frameworks and best practices – all the way down to an instinctual, almost primal level. It's when we find those deeper/unseen needs that our design becomes truly delightful. When I reflect on this matter, my mind immediately goes to Marty Cagan's words from his book *Inspired*: 'Historically, in the vast majority of innovations in our industry, the customers had no idea that what they now love was even a possibility.'[7] Yes, user research can help you understand user needs on a surface level, but you're actually searching for the underlying human emotions that create those needs. Only in this way can you end up creating a seamless and enjoyable experience – one that is not for 'users', but for people, for humans, one that not only touches the surface but brings in new, unpredicted and delightful experiences that improve our lives.

In conclusion, think of UX as a way to touch and positively influence human behaviour and people's day-to-day lives. Many UX professionals I've met during my career go even further and say that UX should, in fact, be called HX, because we can probably say that any user experience we end up creating is part of day-to-day human experience.

There is another level to all this, one that complements what I've just talked about. As designers, every time we create a good user experience, we might think that this is as far as everything goes – we've managed to make one person happy, or one person more confident in their job, or we've simply made someone smile. But for every person touched by a well-designed user experience, there will be others in their proximity who will benefit from this. A person who is pleased by a positive user experience will, without even knowing, pay it forward. Let's think of an example we're all familiar with: a bank clerk who is using an internal application to serve clients. How they experience that tool will reflect in their daily client interactions. If the application is causing frustration, inadvertently, this will have effects on their mood that day, and their confidence levels talking to people, and as we've all probably seen at least once, the stress levels they get exposed to will eventually reflect on us. I like to call this the *UX-sympathetic response* – and it's important because it gives us, designers a lot of distinction, so next time you design a new user experience, think about all this and your responsibilities for making this world a better place, one human experience at a time.

What does good UX 'feel' like?

You know that expression, 'It just feels right'? Well, that's a pretty good description of what makes for great UX. Whether you're browsing a website or using an app on your smartphone, a good user experience should feel 'out of the way' and intuitive. You shouldn't need to waste time fiddling with settings, wondering what button to press or trying to remember where you accessed the menu last time. Everything you need should just be right there, and it should feel natural. Good UX is about anticipating user actions and making sure the interface provides all of the information that's required in a clear, concise way. If you need to restart your thinking process each time you open an app or website, then chances are that the user experience isn't very good.

When UX is done well, you feel like you almost don't need to think about what you're doing. You just *know* how to use the product or website because it flows with your intuition. You don't need to consult the manual; you don't need the FAQ, and a support page sounds like something from a distant past. When designing a product and the interactions and user interface that power it, please keep all this in mind. Make sure you are solving a real user problem by doing solid user research, try to touch the user on a deeper human level by understanding what drives and motivates them and ensure that the UI you design is beautiful, functional, but, most importantly, that it doesn't take centre stage. The UI should *support* the user experience, not *be* the user experience.

You might be wondering why I am telling you all this? Where am I going with it? Yes, it's important, but how can you use this information? What I would like you to remember is one thing: having the understanding of how UX 'feels' to a human will allow you to stand out from the crowd and become a top designer, and that is what your end goal should always be. This will draw the line between a designer that is good enough and an expert in the industry.

As a design expert, you will have better access to the type of projects you love, you will have the opportunity to work with some of the top talent in the field and, last but not least, it will open the way for better financial compensation over time. Love the craft and it will reward you!

Notes

1   D Norman and J Nielsen. The definition of user experience (UX), NN/g, nd. www.nngroup.com/articles/definition-user-experience (archived at https://perma.cc/5T2T-K6MV)

2   Stanford. Steve Jobs' 2005 Stanford commencement address, YouTube, 8 March 2008. youtube.com/watch?v=UF8uR6Z6KLc (archived at https://perma.cc/3H4S-T9RV)

3   J H Stramler (1993) *The Dictionary for Human Factors/Ergonomics*, CRC Press, Boca Raton

4   H Dreyfuss (1955) *Designing for People*, University of California, Los Angeles

5 D Norman and J Nielsen. The definition of user experience (UX), NN/g, nd. www.nngroup.com/articles/definition-user-experience (archived at https:// perma.cc/NYX6-JPKB)

6 H Loranger. UX without user research is not UX, NN/g, 10 August 2014. www. nngroup.com/articles/ux-without-user-research (archived at https://perma. cc/7RLR-ELHF)

7 M Cagan (2018) *Inspired: How to create products customers love*, John Wiley & Sons Inc., Hoboken, New Jersey

CHAPTER TWO

The importance of UX in today's world

The business world is ever-changing, and in order to stay ahead of the competition businesses must always be on the lookout for new opportunities. One such opportunity that can give a business a competitive advantage is investing in UX. In today's digital age, having an effective UX design has become not only essential for creating successful products and services but the norm amongst products that customers actually want to use. Customers today expect that they will enjoy the products they are paying for. This is no longer a 'nice to have', it's a must-have. Businesses that are looking to maximize their future opportunities need to learn why UX is so important and what they should do to make sure their brand stands out from the rest. If you're a designer supporting a business, this is even more important.

Good user experience is clearly good for business. Studies show that companies that invest in UX see a lower cost of customer acquisition, lower support cost, increased customer retention and increased market share, according to a study done by Forrester. When compared to their peers, the top 10 companies leading in customer experience outperformed the S&P index with close to triple the returns. Forrester Research shows that, on average, every dollar invested in UX brings 100 dollars in return.[1]

In addition to creating user-centric solutions for complex problems, UX also ensures that users are given an enjoyable experience each time they interact with a brand, which in return increases customer loyalty. By understanding the value of having UX as a strategic tool, businesses can thrive. While it may take some effort and initial work, investing in UX is well worth it.

In this chapter we'll dive into the elements that make UX a powerful and indispensable tool for successful businesses and look into some recommendations on what they should do to make sure their brand stands out in a noisy market.

Why UX matters: The business case for investing in good design

Without UX, the digital business landscape would be a chaotic and confusing place. Imagine what it would be like to try and navigate through your favourite app if no thought had been put into its design; it would be an endless maze of screens with no clear path or direction, or a collection of features, as some like to say. Or imagine trying to use a product only designed around the needs of the company rather than those of the user – you'd have difficulty understanding how it works and feel frustrated it doesn't actually do what you need it to do. That is why UX is essential for creating successful products and services.

Whenever I think about the risk-reducing aspect of UX, my thoughts immediately go to a quote from Dr Ralf Speth (ex-CEO of Jaguar Land Rover) that summarizes this: 'If you think good design is expensive, you should look at the cost of bad design.'[2] Dr Speth wasn't referring to digital products when he said this, but the same principle can be 100 per cent applied to our field. Yes, as a business you can choose not to invest in UX to save money, but there's a hidden cost attached to that – losing potential customers. Good UX, on the other hand, focuses on providing user-centric solutions for some of the most complex problems – making sure that each feature is easy to understand and fits the customer's behaviour and goals seamlessly. In return, investing in good design can help businesses gain a competitive advantage in their respective markets as customers will be drawn to great user experiences.

Understanding user behaviour and goals is crucial. This can be achieved through user research, testing and the evaluation of analytics data. By understanding in-depth how users interact with a product, businesses can make informed decisions on how to improve that product, improve its UX and eventually increase their profits.

Another important aspect is the ability to provide a consistent user experience across all platforms, because UX can 'zoom in and out' to provide a holistic view on how every element ties together across multiple products and user journeys. This has a very high importance in terms of business strategy, because knowing and mapping how a very complex system works can give the business the ability to pivot or weight efforts on a specific channel depending on marketing conditions or competitor moves. A good real-life example is ensuring that a product is accessible and easy to use on all devices and browsers, including desktop, mobile and tablet. As more and more customers are accessing products and services on their mobile devices, it's important that the user experience is optimized for these devices. You can only do this if you understand the bigger picture and take advantage of the holistic approach UX can give you.

Last but not least, UX can be used in reducing the risk for businesses in terms of building the wrong product by incorporating user research and testing throughout the product development process. This can help companies understand the needs and wants of their target audience, and ensure that the product being built aligns with those needs. This factor has been brilliantly highlighted by Roger Pressman in his book about software engineering: 'For every dollar spent to resolve a problem during product design, $10 would be spent on the same problem during development, and multiply to $100 or more if the problem had to be solved after the product's release.'[3]

So why does the cost of solving user problems increases exponentially during the product life cycle? The answer is simple: once engineering is involved, teams are ramped up and the product goes into full development, changes start becoming very costly. Even a small logic change in a feature can be quite time-consuming and the impact can be tenfold, considering that work might need to be done at both the back-end and front-end levels, regression tests need to be performed and we might have created inflexions in data. Imagine product development is like a big ship (no, not the *Titanic*!) that is capable of doing amazing manoeuvres once it's at the optimal speed. There is just only one small problem: big ships are hard to steer.

In conclusion – make sure you take full advantage in the discovery and early design phase from the product life cycle by using all the tools within UX's remit. It will allow your business to test and validate hypotheses with users without the need to write a single line of code. In return this reduces waste, and the company can focus more resources when it's actually needed. Simply put: UX saves money.

For businesses who want to maximize their future opportunities, the advice here is simple: make sure you invest in UX. For UX designers working for any company: make sure your stakeholders understand the value of UX. It's your responsibility.

FIGURE 2.1   The cost of change in the product life cycle

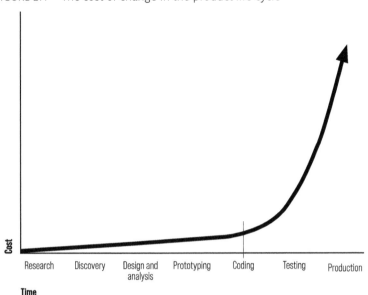

The role of UX design in creating successful products

UX design is a key factor in the success of any product, whether it's a website, app or physical item. It can ensure that users have an enjoyable experience with their favourite product and the business has an advantage over their competitors. Next, we will explore in-depth the role of UX design in creating successful products and provide examples and advice on what approach they should take when designing new user experiences.

Business goals alignment

As mentioned throughout this book, UX design is all about creating user experiences that are tailored to customer needs, expectations and goals. A UX designer should focus on understanding the user's journey and making sure each step of the process is as simple, intuitive and enjoyable as possible. You've probably heard this a few times by now, so it's time to get to work, right? Not so fast! There is an essential step that many UX professionals seem to overlook when they start working on a new product or feature: *business goals alignment*.

Perhaps the most important thing about UX in today's digital world (often omitted or not emphasized enough) is aligning the user experience with the business goals. By all means, the design and functionality of a product should be tailored to meet the needs of your users, but have you thought about meeting the needs of your business? This is where UX design can make a huge difference. A good UX designer should be able to identify how each feature and design decision might affect the business in terms of revenue, cost savings or any other metric really. Without business alignment, you run the risk of creating a product that may be loved by users but not bring any return on investment. Yes, it ends with users, but it *starts* with the business.

So, before you go diving into user research, workshops or wireframing user interfaces, make sure you understand first what your stakeholders and business are trying to achieve. What is their strategy? How is this product or feature going to fit into that strategy? What are the end goals, and what are their short-term and long-term expectations? All this is key to a healthy discovery and design process and it will save resources down the line.

User retention

Another important area where UX plays a key role in creating successful products is user retention (which in a non-technical sense means increased customer satisfaction). The ability to retain users is crucial for the success of a business. This means providing a positive user experience that keeps users engaged and coming back to the product or app you've designed. A good user experience can help improve customer retention. This can then lead to repeat business, positive word-of-mouth(which is critical for social media presence), and increased brand recognition. We're going to look more in-depth at how we create effective user experiences in Part Two of this book.

Cost savings

It doesn't matter how great your ideas are, or how eye-catching and engaging that UI you've just designed is, if they don't match the user needs or the business's goals. If a product is misaligned with its users' needs or with your business's objectives, then it can do only one thing: fail. And when it fails, your business loses money. That is why UX design is a crucial factor in achieving financial success for businesses. As I have mentioned more than once, by understanding and anticipating user needs during the design process, businesses can save resources by avoiding unnecessary development or re-designs that require more time and money.

Staying relevant

Finally, staying relevant in a rapidly changing business world isn't easy. If businesses invest in UX design, they can make sure that their products and services stay ahead of the curve. By understanding user needs and behaviour and adapting to them quickly, businesses can ensure their continued success. Investing in UX design may seem daunting now, but it's the best way to stay competitive.

Notes

1 A Kucheriavy. Good UX is good business: How to reap its benefits, Forbes, 19 November 2015. www.forbes.com/sites/forbestechcouncil/people/ andrewkucheriavy (archived at https://perma.cc/9GHG-DREB)

2   J Short. 5 design quotes that illustrate modern UX practices, Maze, April 30,
    2020. maze.co/blog/design-quotes (archived at https://perma.cc/F5Z7-HG8X)
3   R S Pressman (2010) *Software Engineering: A practitioner's approach*, 7th edn,
    McGraw-Hill, New York

CHAPTER THREE

The future of UX

I n recent years, technology has advanced at an astonishing rate. Each day, new and innovative solutions are being developed that have the potential to reshape the way we live and think about work. From artificial intelligence (AI) to blockchain technology to virtual reality (VR) and extended reality (XR), these emerging technologies are revolutionizing industries across the globe. Not only do these technologies have significant economic implications, they also have the potential to improve the quality of life for people all across the world. In this chapter we will explore some of these technologies and their potential implications for the future of UX design as a discipline. These new technologies will change how UX designers create experiences, how users interact with products and how businesses interact with customers. There are also risks associated with misusing these new technologies and later in the chapter we'll consider how they can be addressed in order to make sure that their positive potential is not lost.

Emerging technologies and their impact on UX

Artificial intelligence

Perhaps the biggest theme these days in terms of emerging technologies is AI, and its implications for the discipline of user experience are considerable. AI technologies such as language models, natural language processing (NLP), computer vision, generative adversarial networks (GANs), etc., are all set to shake up how we design and interact with digital products in the future.

As a UX designer, you will need to be ready and embrace these changes if you want to future-proof your skills and remain relevant in the job market. AI technologies will enable smarter, more personalized interactions with users, voice interfaces will become more ubiquitous and easier to use, and virtual/augmented reality may just be the future of how we interact with digital products. One thing will not change, though: the core principles of UX will still be the same no matter the technology we use or design for – user centricity, accessibility, usability, and consistency will still form the backbone of every great design. No matter what the target output is, it always pays off to start from the basics, and that is a timeless strategy. So, while you do need to learn and adapt, remember that human nature is less likely to change over time. Use that knowledge to design the best possible user experiences that are adapted to the current realities in terms of technology.

Blockchain

Another narrative that can be seen as a potential disruptor to the UX discipline is blockchain – still a hot topic in the technology world. It will certainly have an impact on how we use and perceive money and transactions in the future. Blockchain technology has challenged the very definitions of value and scarcity. While in the physical world these have tangible definitions, in the digital world they push the boundaries of what is possible or even acceptable. By providing the underlying infrastructure for modern data transactions, blockchain technology opens up a whole new realm of possibilities for UX designers to explore. Think about decentralized applications and systems that, instead of being run by companies or groups of people, are run by automated decentralized nodes. Think about designing social media applications that are censorship resistant, where the system can self-regulate rather than be 'managed' by individuals, thus removing the ability of people to 'game the system' or bend the rules. In any case, since the end user is still the focus, user experience will still need to be at the core of this technology.

Internet of Things

The Internet of Things (IoT) is another good example which has the potential to revolutionize how we interact with both physical and digital products, making them smarter and more connected to our everyday life. Devices like wearable health monitors, smart thermostats, home security cameras, smart lighting systems and smart home assistant speakers have become part of our daily routines. UX will be crucial in this domain because it is necessary to map out and understand how the entire system works together as a single user experience. An individual sensor can automatically gather information, can send that data to a device, and then an application installed on that device can analyse all data gathered from many other sources and even cross-link with other devices. All this paints a very complex picture, but in fact what matters the most is final user experience. Who are we using this technology for? What are their goals, and what type of information do they need, and presented in what form? All questions you are familiar with by now. All questions answered by UX.

Virtual reality

As virtual reality technology continues to evolve, UX designers must be prepared for how this will affect users interacting with products and services. By using AR/VR/XR technologies, UX designers can create more immersive experiences that take advantage of the potential of these new ways of interacting. Similarly, the concept of 'metaverse' is beginning to take shape, and users will be able to shape their own virtual environments and interact with others in an entirely unique way. Again, the key principles of UX will be preserved – users first.

As a UX designer, you'll need to think about how these technologies can be used to create better experiences for users. Will users be able to interact with products simply by talking to them? Will they need to learn an entirely new way of interacting with physical objects, or will the interaction remain essentially the same but perhaps the way of processing that interaction will be different? All these questions and more must be taken into account when thinking about how UX can use these new technologies.

Will AI eventually replace me?

If you're like me, you've probably asked yourself this question more than once. Will I end up being replaced by AI? For a very long time, AI has been this abstract concept that we've only seen in movies or read about in the latest sci-fi novel. We've all heard about it, and read about it, but it was always this distant 'thing'. It was always more part of the future than the present, something that is nice to think about but is not actually part of our lives. This made it almost impossible for people to understand it, particularly for those that are not domain experts (so, most of us). But then, something magical happened.

AI really opened up for the first time and started to touch our day-to-day lives. Wherever it was the latest self-driving Tesla car or a new OpenAI language model, or the latest image generation AI, they took the world by storm, and it kind of happened overnight. Yes, the development of AI technology took many, many years, but its adoption happened in an instant. Partly because it was something new, and humans are, by nature, explorers, so they wanted to try out this shiny new thing, but also partly because user experience is now a mature discipline, and the way these tools were presented to the user this time was done by taking advantage of solid UX principles. It was probably the first time that innovators weren't presenting the world with a *technology*, but were presenting the world with a *new experience*. The paradigm has shifted from 'Let me explain to you what AI is' to 'How would you feel about talking to an AI right now?'

The experience of enjoying the ride at the wheel without actually needing to drive, or the experience of asking an AI questions, or generating images from a text prompt, was made available to the public for the first time, and this changed everything.

But, back to where we started. Is AI going to replace you? Is UX a safe job? Or will we have AI-generating user interfaces faster and better than we could ever do? To answer that, think about what design is at its core. Design is about problem-solving and creating delightful experiences for people. I would argue that AI can help us become even better designers by giving us time back through completing any repetitive tasks and mundane work *for us*. That time can now be spent on the things we're even better at, like activities that require creativity and lateral thinking.

So, no, I don't think AI is going to replace UX designers, or any other job that requires creativity, anytime soon. Whenever a new technology has entered the market and hit critical mass, historically it has always been met with fear and anxiety. It's also human nature to fear the unknown. On this very topic, Jerry

Levine, an experienced in-house attorney and AI technology evangelist, observes:

> Clearly, the more corporate leaders adopt AI technology and embrace collaborative intelligence, the more smart machines will change the way work gets done and who ultimately completes it. AI workers can use their multiplied power to handle the mundane parts of people's jobs – complementing human intelligence – and human workers will be able to use their own extraordinary set of skills to push the boundaries of creativity and critical thinking.[1]

UX design specializes in understanding user needs, goals and behaviour. This requires a deep knowledge of the user's lifestyle, environment and context. AI-driven technologies are currently not capable of capturing this information, nor can they design experiences tailored to an individual. Designers are able to develop creative solutions that bridge digital products with real-world experiences, something that AI is unable to do because it lacks the intuition and imagination to create an emotionally engaging experience that resonates with people. As I explained in Chapter 1, understanding human emotions can not only make you a better designer, it will also open up the opportunity to create more meaningful human experiences. Being able to understand the nuances of human emotions and behaviour, and being capable of anticipating how a human thinks, is beyond what AI can do, but it's something *we* can always get better at. So, what for some might seem like our weakness – our emotions – can end up being an even more important part of our lives.

Ultimately, AI is just a tool. AI was not designed to replace us, it was designed to enhance the way we interact with the surrounding world by evolving the way we learn, work or have fun.

Don't worry, design is here to stay.

Some humble predictions for the future

I won't pretend to be a descendant of Nostradamus here. My predictions are just based on my past experience and some logical assumptions I'll be making. Like any predictions, they can be wrong, so forgive me, future reader, if what I'll say here does not make sense anymore. Still, I'll take my chances!

One thing is for certain – the future of UX is going to be exciting. We're entering a world where AI, NLP and VR will play an ever-increasingly important role in how we design user experiences and how people, in return, will interact with them. The challenge for designers will be to combine these technologies with fundamental principles and established methodology so that the experiences we end up creating do indeed improve the lives of people. In the future, it will be easy to fall into the trap of using technology just for the sake of technology. As emerging technologies reach the mainstream, it will be more and more tempting for designers to start using them. Why not use some AI in our app, right? Everyone else is. Ask yourself, are you designing for people's needs, or are you designing to fit a technology? If the answer is the latter, then you aren't doing such a great job.

AI-powered tools have already made it possible to simulate user behaviour in ways that weren't possible before, allowing us to understand our customers better and create more intuitive designs, but, as I said in Chapter 1, UX without the user is *not* UX. This is one thing that will not change in the future. No matter how much technology evolves, you cannot simply replace real behavioural data, because it is so unique. It's linked to human emotions, needs and goals, and the context can change everything.

On the other hand, we can expect a lot more automation. AI-assisted UX design is already here in different shapes or forms, and it is likely to become even more common in the near future. More automation will allow designers to focus on the more creative aspects of UX, with AI taking care of more prosaic tasks. Imagine running user research interviews but not having to manually analyse the data after. What if an AI could summarize findings and automatically create the main themes across multiple interviews and maybe even come up with recommendations? This will allow you to perform research faster than ever, and maybe even perform automated deep research, combining both quantitative and qualitative data to extract insights automatically. In return, you can probably focus more on the product vision, the interactions and improving usability.

Another prediction I have for the future is that we will mix technologies that today we consider cutting edge in a way that will enable products to become much easier to use, and our way of interacting with them will feel much more natural. Just imagine using an application without needing a keyboard, a mouse or even a touch screen. What if we could use a combination of voice recognition, gestures (hands, eyes, head), automated lip reading, eye-tracking, etc., all working seamlessly together? It is probably the most natural way we interact with the real world, so why not with a digital product? From a UX perspective, this will, of course, mean an increase in complexity – more services running in parallel, more ways of interpreting data, and most of it in the background without the user even realizing or needing to know an interface is there.

Or perhaps you are more adventurous, and you'll want to try a brain–computer interface to simply circumvent the need for any of the old ways of inputting information. The good news is that we've already witnessed successful experiments in this field, like a paralysed person being able to write using a brain implant, and Elon Musk's Neuralink video showing a monkey playing the game of Pong just by using its mind.[2] But back to inputting information. I said 'old ways' because they are slow. 'Wait, what?' you will say. Hear me out: you were probably inputting information much faster when you were using a keyboard. If you're like me, even with predictive text, on a mobile device you will be significantly slower at typing in data. This represents a huge bottleneck in terms of communication bandwidth. If a computer can send an immense amount of data to you in an instant, we are sending an insignificant amount back by comparison. At best a few words per second. Why does this matter for UX? Because everything we design needs to work in that context, where our speed of inputting and digesting information is a key factor. Brain–computer interfaces will allow us to remove that obstacle and perhaps increase our speed of sending data to a system because you no longer need to type it in – you can just think it, or feel it. This advancement will radically change UX as a discipline, opening up new frontiers in terms of what an interface can do. Perhaps we can also increase our capacity for processing data that is sent from the system. Put these two together and we have the next evolution in sight.

My final prediction has little to do with technology. I predict that no matter how much we'll advance in terms of new technologies, one thing will not change: humans will still be emotion-driven – and that is where UX is at its best. Being able to research, analyse and understand human emotions and everything that goes into our decision-making process will mean that there will always be a place for UX as a discipline, no matter how advanced we are in terms of science and technology.

With that being said, happy future designing!

Notes

1 J Levine. Combining intelligence: How people and AI can collaborate, Forbes, 26 April 2022. www.forbes.com/sites/forbesbusinesscouncil/2022/04/26/ combining-intelligence-how-people-and-ai-can-collaborate (archived at https:// perma.cc/WM96-C3B3)

2 K O'Leary. Handwriting with a brain implant, Nature.com, May 27, 2021. www.nature.com/articles/d41591-021-00036-2 (archived at https://perma. cc/785J-VZYP; J Wakefield. Elon Musk's Neuralink 'shows monkey playing Pong with mind', BBC News, 9 April 2021. www.bbc.co.uk/news/ technology-56688812 (archived at https://perma.cc/V5U9-GL6Q)

The UX design process

Part Two of this book covers the UX design process – what it means, how we execute it, and the core methodologies you need to get acquainted with in order to be successful. We are going to do some deep dives into some of the topics in order to make sure you learn everything you need to get started with UX.

To put it briefly, UX design is a process that involves understanding user behaviours, motivations and needs in order to create a product or service that meets their expectations. But, as we discussed in Chapter 2, this is not enough. We also need to take into account the business goals and the financial and technical realities that give context to our product. UX design focuses on the entire experience of using a product or service, covering all aspects of the end user's journey. This includes how users are onboarded, how they interact with the content, look at visuals, navigate websites and applications, as well as how they interpret messages within an interface. Designers must understand the behaviour of their users in order to develop solutions that transform any experience into a delightful one. By taking into account user research, data analysis and feedback from stakeholders UX designers can successfully craft experiences that match customers' needs while satisfying business objectives.

In Part Two we will take a closer look at the UX design process and some of the core methodologies needed to get started with UX. We will discuss user research and research methodologies, design thinking, data-driven UX, interaction design basics and UI design principles. We'll finish off with advice on how to evaluate designs and learn about UX strategy and its role in navigating complex organizations. So sit back, relax and let's learn how to create the most amazing user experiences.

CHAPTER FOUR

A linear view of a non-linear process

U X design is often presented as a linear process, with clear steps that neatly go from one to the next. But anyone who's ever tried to design something knows it's not that straightforward. As you can imagine, there are no straight lines in UX design! The reality is that *UX design is non-linear and iterative* – while you might start by researching user needs and then move on to ideation, wireframes and prototypes, chances are you'll be going back and forth between these stages more than once. It's also not uncommon for designers to find themselves tinkering over interactions even after the product has been launched! This is because UX does not live in a vacuum – it's influenced by business realities, finances, changes in user behaviour, etc. The world works in cycles, so it only makes sense for UX to mimic that.

Non-linear design allows for flexibility, which can be great when trying to accommodate user research findings, business goals and creative ideas. It's also helpful to keep in mind that the finished product is likely never going to be perfect – rather, it's an ongoing process of improvement (this is where the iterative part of design comes into play). After all, what you think will work for your users now may not hold up to their expectations tomorrow. Believe it or not, that is a good thing. That is how we evolve.

So, the next time you're presented with a linear UX design process, remember: it's not always so simple! Keep an open mind, and don't be afraid to try out new ideas – because when it comes down to it, design is all about exploring solutions and pushing boundaries so your users end up with the best possible experience they can get. That means being willing to sometimes take some risks and go against what many would consider standard practices! If there is one constant in design, it's self-improvement.

A non-linear, iterative process

Linear, non-linear, iterative, cyclical – I know, you're confused, right? Let me explain. Have a look at Figure 4.1. It's a high-level

FIGURE 4.1   Illustrating UX design as a linear process

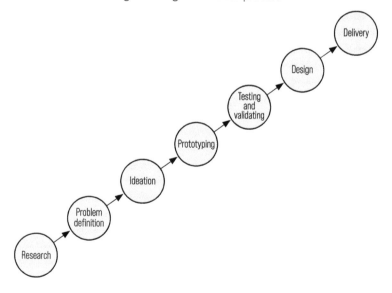

diagram of a linear UX process. I know, I know – I told you that UX is non-linear. Hear me out. UX design is often presented as a linear process, but in reality it's anything but. From user research to high-fidelity prototyping and everything in between, UXers know that design is an iterative process of trial and error. Sure, there are certain best practices that guide us along the way – such as user-centred design principles – but at its core UX design is a non-linear process.

So why do we persist in presenting UX design as a linear process? Well, simplicity plays a big role here. It's much easier to explain the basics of UX using linear steps than trying to convey the complex interplay of elements involved with non-linear UX design processes. On top of that, creating timelines and checklists can be helpful for beginners in organizing and prioritizing their tasks. So, to put it simply: we're doing it on purpose so it's easier for you to understand.

FIGURE 4.2   Illustrating UX design as a non-linear iterative process

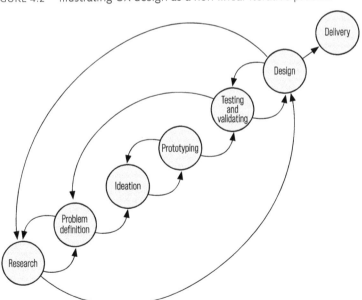

So how does the UX process actually look in reality? I thought you'd never ask. Figure 4.2 is probably a much closer representation of the reality of UX design processes.

Well, you asked for it, and I delivered! Do you see the problem here? The closer we get to trying to visualize the actual complexity of the UX design process, the more we lose your attention. Tough position to be in, no?

Also, I said *much closer* to reality, because in the real world, in many cases it's more like Figure 4.3.

Ok, now we're talking! Do I have your attention? Yes, this is probably how this process works in real life. Surprised? Don't be. Life isn't a linear process. The way people interact with products isn't linear either. It's organic, based on their day-to-day needs. Humans don't think and act in a linear way, so why should design be linear? If anything, it's one of the most adaptable and open-to-change disciplines there is. At the end of the

FIGURE 4.3   Illustrating UX design as an organic, real-life like process

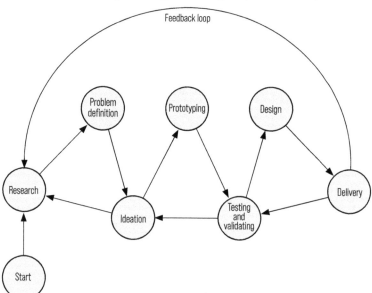

day, as UX designers, you must remember that non-linearity is an integral part of any creative process. You have to be flexible enough to make changes on the fly, adapt your solutions as needed, and think outside the box when it comes to finding new ideas. That's how UX works best! So instead of following a linear path, embrace complexity – because, after all, great design comes from unexpected places. With time that's something you'll understand better than anyone else!

Not only can this help prevent us from getting stuck in a rut, but it also gives us room to explore new solutions and uncover hidden opportunities by walking the unknown path. Fundamentally, UX design is a creative process, and creativity thrives when it's allowed to move freely. So the next time you embark on a design journey, don't be deterred by a non-linear route! You never know what discoveries await.

Iterate, iterate, iterate

The UX design process is iterative because designers need to continuously adapt and refine the user experience based on new data, user feedback and insights from business stakeholders. Through this iterative approach, you can ensure that the products you're working on meet the needs of users while also meeting business objectives.

The process typically begins with research, where through interviews we gather data about users, the product or service we are designing for and the context in which it will be used. This helps us inform the design decisions that come afterwards. Designers then create wireframes and prototypes to test out different ideas before producing a 'final', more polished version of the product or service. I say 'final' because UX being an iterative process – we never have an absolutely final design. We also talk about a particular state, a milestone in a timeline, if you wish. Once that milestone is reached, this is tested again with users to identify areas for improvement and make changes accordingly.

UX designers know that there's a lot more to designing a great user experience than just having a good eye or being creative. A lot of it is about the process. And when it comes to UX design, there's no better way to go about it than with an iterative approach. Iterations are essential for UX design because they allow us to make adjustments and improvements along the way as we get feedback from our users and stakeholders. This allows us to tweak and refine our designs until we hit the sweet spot where everyone is happy with the outcome. Plus, by taking an iterative approach, we can reduce risks for businesses – who doesn't want that, right?

Moreover, iteration helps designers get creative by allowing them to try different things and see what works best. Iteration also allows us to spot potential issues early on in the process before they become bigger problems, thereby saving time and money down the line. Given the complexity of designing a user experience, is it even reasonable to think we can do it perfectly from the very beginning? Or should we even try? Let's look at what Jakob Nielsen, co-founder of NN/g, has to say about this:

> It has long been recognized that user interfaces should be designed iteratively in almost all cases because it is virtually impossible to design a user interface that has no usability problems from the start. Even the best usability experts cannot design perfect user interfaces in a single attempt, so a usability engineering lifecycle should be built around the concept of iteration.[1]

There is one more element I want to bring to your attention. Iterative design is not easy to digest. It will definitely test you and push you towards your limits, mentally. Why do I say this? As an aspiring UX designer, you will try to do all the right things and perhaps reach a point where you think you have the perfect solution and maybe even get to design it. But then, stakeholders change their mind, engineering discovers potential blockers, user feedback is negative, or perhaps the product manager has a shift in strategy. And that 'perfect' design is gone! What I'm trying to say is that things change all the time. At first, you will be uncomfortable and unfamiliar with the feeling. The more you progress in your career, the better you will get to know yourself and will be able to control your initial impulse – which is to be resistant to change or, worse, take change personally. Try to remember one thing: this is not about you! It's about doing the right thing for your users.

At the end of the day, UX design is a process that requires patience, resilience and lots of diplomacy. But when done right this process can lead to great user experiences that keep our users coming back for more. So, my advice is – embrace the iterative nature of UX design!

The balancing act of user needs, business goals and technology

We've learned how the UX process looks at a high-level, how iterations are important for design and that we might have some iterating to do on ourselves if we want to progress in this field. Ultimately, UX design is a balancing act between the needs of users, business goals and technology. I've carefully chosen the word 'balancing' because I think it perfectly describes how UX needs to be performed.

When it comes to UX design, building alignment between user needs and business goals helps create an optimal experience for the user. UX designers must seek to understand what both parties need from each other in order to bridge the gap between them. *UX should ensure that business objectives are met while keeping user needs as a priority.* I can't stop emphasizing the importance of this aspect. During my career, I've seen so many designers that simply miss this point. User-centred design doesn't mean you can ignore the business goals or even that they are someone else's responsibility.

There's a third variable in this equation: technology (engineering). Often overlooked, technology plays a major role in UX design. UX designers must have expertise in the capabilities of their platforms and how to exploit them in order to provide the best possible user experience. Also, we need to make sure the engineering team is not just presented with final designs and instructions, but rather is part of the entire design process from start to finish. When used correctly, this partnership can create amazing user experiences. Involving engineers in UX design early on helps define all the technical constraints and ensures that a realistic approach is taken for each project. As UX designers, we should never under-estimate the importance of our engineering teams and how they can influence the outcome of final product.

FIGURE 4.4   Good UX takes place at the intersection of user needs, business goals and technical capabilities

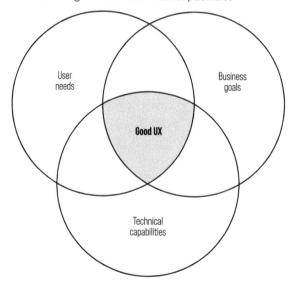

In summary, UX design is a process of understanding user needs, business objectives and technical constraints. UX designers must have an in-depth knowledge of their target audience, their behaviour and preferences, as well as the technology available to deliver solutions, and match these with the business goals. UX designers need to constantly evaluate what users need in terms of experience, and how it can be delivered effectively and efficiently within budget constraints, as well as account for any technical limitations that may exist. Of course, all this requires UX practitioners to have a good grasp of UX methodologies, technology and business.

Good UX happens at the intersection of user needs, business goals and technological constraints. It's only when we balance these three things, we can truly create the best user experiences.

I know what you're going to say. 'But, you've already told me all this.' Ok, hear me out. I just want to make sure you understand what they *really* mean, so let's take a closer look.

User needs

Ok, this one should be simple. We perform research, ask users what they need, capture it and design it, right? Well, not exactly. Let me tell you why. It's important to understand the subtle difference between user needs and user wants. Many designers, product managers or stakeholders seem to misinterpret this, and it can have disastrous consequences. The difference between the two might indeed be subtle, but translated into a user experience, it can be worlds apart.

So what is the difference? User *needs* are the result of carefully collected and analysed user research. We listen to what our users have to say, what they feel, and what their goals are, and then, using all our knowledge, we put all that through the lens of user experience. Needless to say, this step will require knowledge from different areas, such as user research, behavioural science, data analysis, etc. We interpret what they say and we draw conclusions. User *wants*, on the other hand, are the users' demands. We listen to users, note down what they ask for and proceed to deliver them. We do not analyse user research data, or pass it through any critical thinking lens; we use the data in its raw form. This can be extremely damaging to a product. Imagine it this way: when utilizing user needs, you are the designer; when utilizing user wants, they are the designer. I'll go into more detail on this topic in Chapter 5.

Business goals

It's a UX designer's dream to create products that delight and engage users, but without business goals UX design is nothing more than a pipe dream. Business goals are the foundation for successful products, and they provide designers with the necessary boundaries to keep the focus on what is important. Failing to consider business goals in your user experience can have catastrophic consequences for that product.

Without satisfying the business goals, UX designers risk creating solutions that don't align with market movements. This could lead to a product that fails to meet customer demands or adds little value to the company – resulting in a waste of time and resources. We've learned that UX solutions must be backed up by facts from research or data analysis; not having clear business objectives means there might be no way to measure if the design you're proposing is achieving its purpose.

It's important that UX designers understand the objectives of their business and how UX can help to achieve them, so they can create products that both meet user needs and deliver value to the business. For this, you need to be able to operate at both the tactical and strategic levels, switching when necessary. Aspiring UX designers should familiarize themselves with the market and industry trends, as well as take the proper time to research their company's objectives and have stakeholder interviews before embarking on a UX project. This will ensure a successful outcome for everyone involved. Only doing user research is not enough.

Ultimately, UX design without business goals is like steering a ship when the passengers (your users) haven't indicated a destination – it will only take you in circles and waste precious resources along the way! Taking into account business goals allows UX designers to build solutions that are not only attractive but also profitable and sustainable.

Technology constraints

When thinking about technology constraints, try to imagine two sides to this coin: on one side we have people – engineers that have different sets of skills and are domain experts in different technologies, and on the other side we have the financials – salaries, budgets, operational costs, etc. This is where technology overlaps with business more than it does with UX. As a result, in many companies where the UX maturity is limited, there is a much higher business emphasis put on engineering than on design. This happens for several reasons, but the simplest one is that you cannot have a digital product without code, while everything else is negotiable to the business. So, as UX designers, sometimes we still need to prove the value of our discipline. We have all heard about UX designers and engineers working together in perfect harmony to bring to life great products or service. However, this symbiosis rarely exists in practice due to mismatched expectations from both parties.

From an engineering perspective, UX designers can often come up with ideas that are not feasible from a tech standpoint. This means UX designers must get better at understanding how their designs will work with the underlying tech architecture and how much effort is required for the engineering team to implement their solutions. On the other hand, engineering teams may overlook user needs and prioritize speed or convenience over user experience – sacrificing usability for optimization or short-term gains, which causes poor results in terms of user experience.

Designs that don't consider tech feasibility end up not being developed or, worse, impede progress as engineers are left to navigate complex implementations with limited resources. Understanding the engineering side will also make you a better designer. Bringing engineers to the table, making them part of the UX design process, will make you a rock star.

When contemplating the concept of good UX, I often think about a dialogue between the musician Tom Waits and film-maker Jim Jarmusch that brilliantly surfaces the fact that creative work is also about balance:

> Jim Jarmusch once told me fast, cheap, and good… pick two. If it's fast and cheap, it won't be good. If it's cheap and good, it won't be fast. If it's fast and good, it won't be cheap. Fast, cheap and good… pick two words to live by.[2]

Of course, Jim Jarmusch was referring to the difficulties of making films at the time, but I think we can definitely apply it to product development as well. Table 4.1 puts that into context for you.

So, where am I going with this? That no matter what you do, your product is going to fail? Of course not! Remember what I said – UX is a balancing act. You can never tick off all the boxes completely. Not in real life, anyway. I'm not aware of any scenario where everything happened perfectly, where designers and product managers uncovered all user needs and perfectly matched those with business goals while staying on budget and having the perfect technology stack. It simply does not happen. In real life, there will be a constant negotiation between these three variables. A constant trade. Balance!

So grab your UX hat, saddle up, and get ready for an adventure!

TABLE 4.1   The impact of technology constraints on UX design outcomes

User Needs	Business Goals	Technical Constraints	Outcome
✔	✔	✘	You will likely exceed the budget expectations, or, even worse, it will be too technically complex to build.
✔	✘	✔	This product has little chance of seeing the light of day.
✘	✔	✔	You might build this, but it will very likely end up in a failure.
✔	✔	✔	'One of the basic rules of the universe is that nothing is perfect. Perfection simply doesn't exist. Without imperfection, neither you nor I would exist.' (Stephen Hawking)

Notes

1   J Nielsen J (1993) Iterative user interface design, NN/g, 1 November 1993. www.nngroup.com/articles/iterative-design (archived at https://perma.cc/2BW6-S9B7)

2   P Maher Jr (2011) *Tom Waits on Tom Waits: Interviews and encounters*, Chicago Review Press, Chicago

CHAPTER FIVE

The foundations of UX

Understanding user needs

As you've learned in the previous chapters, UX involves much more than just producing a visually appealing product or website. As designers, we must understand the needs of our users in order to create an effective and enjoyable experience. UX is founded on the principle that user needs should be at the core of the design process (user centricity), and these needs should be consistently monitored throughout development. Together, we will explore the foundations of UX by examining how UX designers are able to identify and address user needs. We'll look at UX research methods, such as interviews and surveys, and learn how understanding a user's motivations can inform better design decisions. Finally, we'll look at how UX research sits at the heart of problem-solving frameworks such as design thinking, and how to perform a successful discovery process to ensure users' and business needs are met. By exploring these topics, I hope you'll be in a much better position to grasp the importance of user needs in UX design. Let's get started!

What is user research?

I could probably write an entire book dedicated just to user research. It's a complex topic, but let's start with the basics.

User research generally refers to the process of gathering user research data in order to learn more about their needs so that we design products or services that meet those needs. The Interaction Design Foundation defines it as:

> the systematic study of target users and their requirements, to add realistic contexts and insights to design processes. UX researchers adopt various methods to uncover problems and design opportunities. Doing so, they reveal valuable information which can be fed into the design process.[1]

I like their definition because it adds one crucial element – 'target users'. This might seem like a no-brainer, but you would be surprised how many times the users who take part in research are not actually part of the target audience. This usually occurs because there is a gap in communication between the design team, the product team and the business. Not understanding the target audience means that we will target the wrong users. Now think about how useful that data will be. I touched on this point in the previous chapter. Just because you're interviewing users, do it by the book, and follow the process, it doesn't mean you're doing good user research. Not if it's with the wrong users. It's even riskier because all the insights captured get circulated within the team, are shared with the business, and the entire decision-making chain is then affected. So, it's essential to get this step right. Make sure you select the actual target users for your product, and do not compromise on this, even if it's tempting to do so!

There is no 'one size fits all' process for user research – it often involves a combination of techniques and methods. This usually depends on the context. Where in the product life cycle are you? Is it a greenfield initiative (a product developed entirely from scratch) or a mature product? What is the type of application you're developing? Is it native mobile? Is it a responsive website? What is the business context? Is it business-to-consumer (B2C), or perhaps it's an internally facing enterprise app? You get the point. By answering these questions, you will be able to assess and come up with a solid user research strategy, and match the scope of your research to the realities of your product. I can't stress this fact enough, as it's missed by so many designers – be time conscious! User research involves choosing an appropriate method to answer specific questions, all within a given budget and timeline. Don't discount the amount of synthesis needed for each approach when selecting which one is best suited for the initiative at hand. Remember what we discussed in Chapter 1 – UX too late is *not* UX.

In addition to getting insights from user interviews and analytics, user research also plays a role in how teams collaborate and communicate with each other. User research gives team members the opportunity to discuss user-specific issues and brainstorm solutions together. This type of partnership leads to more innovative ideas that help shape the user experience. We'll dive into this topic more a bit later when discussing the discovery process and problem-solving frameworks such as design thinking.

Now that you've understood how you can use research to your advantage to design better products for your users, it's time to have a closer look at the actual process. There are many methods for collecting user research, such as interviews (for both users and stakeholders), surveys, usability testing, A/B testing, journey mapping. In the next section we'll take a deeper dive into some of the most popular methods and discuss when and how to use them, but before then I want to give you a better understanding of how user research methods are categorized. The easiest way to visualize this is probably by aligning each method to the step in the product design life cycle where it's used the most (Figure 5.1). Just to be clear, this is *just one way* of grouping them. In fact, in the next section I will introduce you to a different classification that is based on the type of research. But let's get back to this one now.

As you can see, there are six main steps in a product life cycle: strategy, discovery, design, evaluation, delivery and production. Of course, this assumes a greenfield project, where in reality it's probably very likely that you will find yourself working on a product that has already been launched. I'll try to explain what each of these phases means in more detail and what user research methods are the most effective in each of them.

FIGURE 5.1   User research methods mapped against the product life cycle

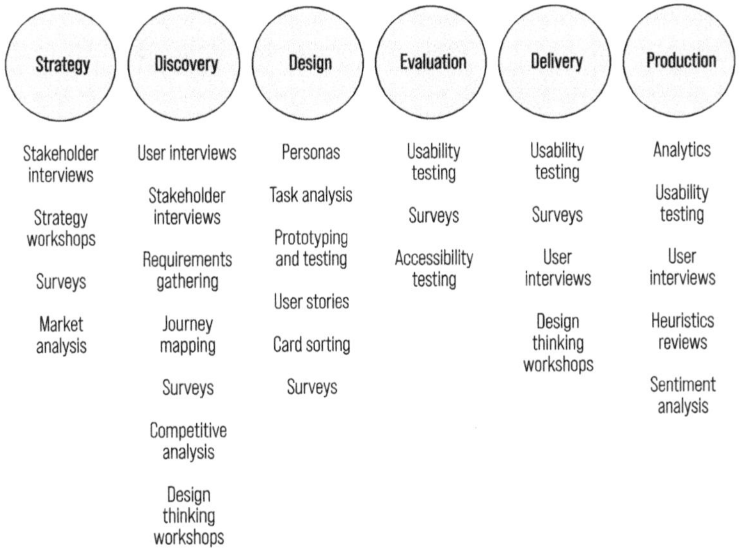

Strategy	Discovery	Design	Evaluation	Delivery	Production
Stakeholder interviews	User interviews	Personas	Usability testing	Usability testing	Analytics
Strategy workshops	Stakeholder interviews	Task analysis	Surveys	Surveys	Usability testing
Surveys	Requirements gathering	Prototyping and testing	Accessibility testing	User interviews	User interviews
Market analysis	Journey mapping	User stories		Design thinking workshops	Heuristics reviews
	Surveys	Card sorting			Sentiment analysis
	Competitive analysis	Surveys			
	Design thinking workshops				

The strategy phase

This is perhaps the most elusive of phases. Why do I say this? Because this is where the ideas are in their infancy. We rarely know when a product actually originates. It's more likely that it's a long-term thinking process for an individual or a small group of business people until they decide to put their ideas into action. UX, in general, is seldom present in this phase, but when it is, it can add tremendous value. Although a rare occurrence, when it does happen, there are a few research methods that you may use, such as strategy workshops, market analysis or stakeholder interviews. I included this phase because UX can add value here through UX strategy by influencing the product vision. It is at this stage that we can lay the foundations for the product's vision. At this point in time we can define the North Star – the aspirational long-term mission of the product – and this will guide everything that happens later. Of course, the product vision gets gradually built over time, notably in the discovery phase, but having UX involved so early in the process means we can make sure user-centricity will be core to this project.

The discovery phase

For greenfield projects, the discovery phase is perhaps the most important in terms of the potential impact on the product. It is within this phase that we define the business goals, ideally accompanied by the entire team (business, design, product and engineering). Perhaps the most important method we can use in this phase is the user interview. A one-to-one conversation with a user is extremely valuable in the discovery process because it allows us to gain deeper insights into people's needs and define how would they interact with the product. Another very similar type of method is the stakeholder interview. Although purely from a technical perspective they are very similar, the end goals are very different. If one is designed to extract data that can be used to inform our solutions, the latter is designed to make sure those solutions sit within certain realistic boundaries. They are both equally important for a successful discovery phase. Another important method we use in this phase is requirements gathering. This is essentially the art of making sense of all the insights and information you've accrued in the discovery phase. I'm calling it an art, because aligning multidisciplinary teams on what's required for a product can sometimes feel like herding cats. Once you learn how to do that, however, it's a UX design superpower. These requirements are the equivalent of laying the groundwork for a building. The better information we have, the more likely our future building will fit this foundation. Requirements gathering allows us to make the transition from conceptual to concrete.

The design phase

The key methods I would like to mention here are personas (artefacts that we use to synthetize user research data into a more digestible form), journey mapping (capturing and visualizing the process a user goes through to achieve a goal) and user stories (foundational elements that will later form the structure of the product backlog, describing, at a high level, the functionality needed by each of the features). While personas are mostly used to reinforce user research findings amongst the team, journey mapping and user stories are used to give shape to the actual product. What is interesting to remember here is that the design phase is usually where most iterations and pivoting can happen. You can have a design phase in the context of a new product, but you can also have it in the context of a new feature or direction within an already established product. Personas, user journeys, story mapping – consider them as fluid. A persona can change based on market conditions or a change in direction of the product (targeting a different audience). User journeys can change based on newly discovered user needs and goals, and user stories will change as a result of that, describing new features and functionality.

The evaluation phase

Also sometimes referred to as the design testing phase, this is where we will evaluate the effectiveness of our design solutions. We'd done the research, ran a successful discovery and proto-typed our solution. But does it actually work? Before we go into development and invest, we always test our solutions with users. The key method used in this phase is the usability test, a form of user research interview that allows us to test prototypes in order to gather initial feedback and validate if our solution is indeed satisfactory for the users. There are multiple variations of the usability test: qualitative/quantitative, remote/in person, moder-ated/unmoderated. The principle behind them is largely the same: we are giving the user a set of tasks to complete and we get a response from them. The difference between the variations comes from how we perform the test and what is the goal of the test. A good example is testing a user interface with a moderated approach. We can test for qualitative data, and find out how the user feels about the design, how they react to it, and what they have to say, or, we can test for quantitative data, testing for example how long a certain task takes them to complete or what is the success rate for a certain action. I will go into a lot more detail regarding the evaluation process in Chapter 8.

The delivery phase

Once our designs are thoroughly validated and the team decides it's time to go into development, the product team will define a minimum viable product (MVP) – which is essentially a set of core features that will allows the user to perform most of their tasks and can produce business value. A successfully defined MVP needs to be both testable and usable in a real-life business scenario. The most common research methods we employ in the delivery phase are user interviews and usability tests. So what is the difference? Technically they are using the same methodology, but what you're testing is no longer a prototype but a real product. That does bring in some extra complexity because you will have to account for the fact that the product is an MVP, so the user will not have access to the entire set of features like they did on the prototype. Even more, they might encounter bugs or unexpected behaviours. While with a prototype you are mostly in control, with an MVP you will have to mitigate lots of factors such as incomplete functionality, performance issues, errors, incomplete data, etc. This is no longer a simulation!

The production phase

Although in theory the MVP is a live product, in practice there is actually a milestone that will mark the completion of the MVP and the beginning of the production phase, and that is when the product team is happy with the core features already implemented. The line between the delivery and production phases is a bit blurred because it depends upon the context. What is an MVP in a B2C start-up might not be classified as an MVP for an internally facing enterprise app, for example. The scope and margins for error will be very different. Another way of looking at this is from an engineering perspective – reaching a stable product. The core features are there, most of the bugs are ironed out and there are no significant changes on the horizon. That is when the product is ready to scale. The most common research methods here are analytics studies, surveys and usability testing. Using these three methods will offer you solid coverage in terms of research data. Analytics and surveys will offer a view into the quantitative data, looking at conversion funnels, usage stats, adoption metrics, etc., while usability testing will allow you to keep an eye on the quality of execution of the UI.

As a key takeaway, please remember that *user research is an essential part of UX* as a discipline. With user research at the centre of your work, you'll be well-positioned to deliver exceptional user experiences every time.

User research methods, or when to do what

By now, you've become familiar with a few user research methods, and we've learned where some of them are likely to occur in the product life cycle. But when exactly do you use which one? How do you decide that? And what are the benefits of using each of them? Next, we will explore how to choose between different user research techniques and when to use them for maximum effect. So, let's learn how to get the most out of your user research!

As we've learned in the previous section, there is a wide array of different methods that we can use, each offering distinct advantages and having various disadvantages, so it can be challenging to know when to use which one. On top of that, the type of user research we need to conduct can also be influenced by the type of product we're trying to build, the environment we plan to run it in or the time and budget we have at our disposal. Knowing when to use what user research methods can be tricky – sometimes, it might even feel like finding a needle in a haystack. One thing I always found helpful was to start with Christian Rohrer's 'Landscape of user research methods'. Christian is a VP of Design at TD Bank Group and an NN/g industry instructor, and authored the framework. This visualization brilliantly categorizes some of the most utilized user research methods by placing them into quadrants on three dimensions (Figure 5.2).

The three dimensions are attitudinal vs behavioural, qualitative vs quantitative and context of product use. These are very useful when selecting the best research method for your product and your particular scenario.

The 'attitudinal vs behavioural' dimension

This dimension can be described as 'what people say' vs 'what people do'. What does this mean? Attitudinal user research is all about understanding people's expressed feelings and opinions towards a product or service. This is important to remember,

FIGURE 5.2 A framework for choosing user research methods: 'The landscape of user research methods'

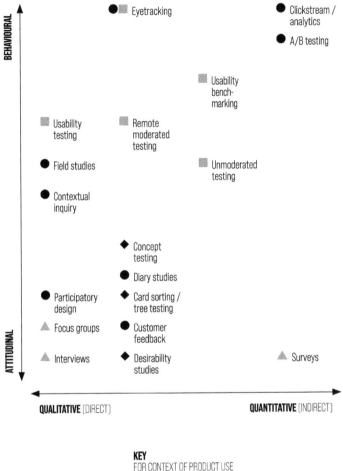

KEY
FOR CONTEXT OF PRODUCT USE
DURING DATA COLLECTION

● Natural use of product

▒ Scripted use of product

▲ Decontextualized (not using the product)

◆ Limited (use of a limited form of the product to study a specific aspect of the user experience)

Source: Christian Rohrer, NN/g

because sometimes people do not want to voice their feelings fully, and this is the main drawback for methods that fit into the attitudinal category. Users will often tend to be friendly and agreeable and generally do not want to 'hurt your feelings' when a delicate topic is addressed. It is essential for a facilitator to make participants feel comfortable and encourage them to express their true beliefs. Unfortunately, in most cases, that will not fully happen.

Attitudinal user research can help uncover how users think and feel when interacting with your product. It usually involves interviews, focus groups or participatory design sessions. By uncovering users' emotions, motivations, frustrations and preferences about your products or services, this type of user research helps identify issues that could be preventing user engagement or satisfaction and spot opportunities for improvements or new features. On the other hand, behavioural user research is more about understanding how people react ('what people do'). Some of the most common methods here are A/B testing, usability testing, eye tracking, etc.

It's not uncommon, for example, for the same participant to react differently to an in-person user interview vs a remote usability testing session. In the user interview, they might be more friendly and diplomatic in an effort not to hurt the facilitator's feelings, whereas in a remote unmoderated test they might feel more inclined to voice their honest thoughts or perform actions that were not revealed in the user interview.

Of course, not all these methods will be fully attitudinal or behavioural. There are nuances. Take, for example, usability testing. Although they are definitely more weighted toward the behavioural end of the scale, it doesn't mean they do not provide attitudinal data.

The 'qualitative vs quantitative' dimension

We can best describe this dimension by the way we gather this data. If qualitative data is mostly gathered directly from the participants (e.g. user interview), quantitative data will be gathered indirectly (e.g. survey). Both qualitative and quantitative methods will also require a great deal of synthesis after the sessions are performed, but that synthesis will be done in two different ways. Qualitative data will generally be synthesized as notes, themes, specific pain points, etc., while quantitative data will use classic data analysis techniques. To put it simply, qualitative methods are more geared towards behavioural elements (e.g. why a user is feeling frustrated when accessing a feature), whereas quantitative methods are more geared towards analytical insights (e.g. how many users have accessed that feature and what was the average session length).

Both qualitative and quantitative research methods provide valuable insight but they are used for very different purposes. For example, qualitative research like interviews or usability testing can help determine *why* something isn't working, while quantitative methods such as surveys yield more tangible data like *how often* or *how many* people are using the product. Each type is important in uncovering important elements that can steer product development in the right direction.

The 'context of product use' dimension

As the title says, this dimension describes the context of the use of the methods. In his framework, Christian Rohr describes this dimension as having four possible buckets:

- *Natural:* The study is performed in a natural environment for the user (e.g. A/B testing, eye tracking).
- *Scripted:* The study uses a predefined script (e.g. usability testing, remote moderated testing).
- *Limited:* The study is using a limited version of the product (e.g. testing an early prototype in participatory design sessions).
- *Decontextualized:* The user is not using the product during the session (e.g. user interviews or surveys).

Overall, user research methods provide invaluable insights that can help you to improve user experience and increase customer satisfaction. Understanding the differences between these dimensions will allow you to choose the most suitable method for your needs – one that will generate the best results in terms of gathering insights and data to improve your product or services. By leveraging all these user research techniques, we can gain an even greater understanding of our users' wants and needs – so don't be afraid to try them out!

What is discovery, and why does it matter?

The discovery phase

The discovery phase in product development involves activities that help the team better understand the problem space, gain insights into user needs and behaviours and come up with design concepts in the solutions space that satisfy both user and business needs.

The discovery process in product development is like planning a holiday. I'm sure you've done that at least once, and it's not an easy job – you need to book the tickets and accommodation, get to the airport in time, have the correct documents with you, have a map and route plan in order to get to your favourite attractions, and take out insurance in case something bad happens. That's a lot of work. Why am I using this analogy? Because without planning, that holiday can become an aimless journey full of frustration and can end up being costly both financially and in terms of time. Similarly, in the UX world, discovery is the essential first step for any product design process, the planning phase, providing direction on user needs, insights into customer behaviour, capturing business goals, research into existing solutions, etc. And just like planning a holiday, it can get quite intense. There isn't necessarily any rulebook in terms of steps you need to take. Generally, following UX best practices in terms of research and planning, and potentially using a problem-solving framework such as design thinking (I'll go into more details on that in the next section), can help make it a more structured process. But, be ready for change, because that's what discovery is – an opportunity to keep things fluid and organic. It will give you a chance to explore multiple routes and test multiple solutions. You will have to use all your skills (and energy) to extract insights, present them back and convince your stakeholders to go with a particular solution. All this is incredibly hard work, but at the same time it's incredibly rewarding. If done well it represents the difference between a successful product and a failure. All you need to do is embrace chaos!

The Discovery phase of a product isn't just about getting a sense of *what* needs to be done; it's also about understanding *why* something needs to be done, which can often lead to discovering new opportunities that weren't previously thought possible. Discovery typically involves activities such as user interviews, data analysis, stakeholder interviews, participatory design sessions and more. This is a great way to get the complete picture before jumping into development, which can get really expensive really quickly, as I explained in the previous chapter. Having an open discovery process by involving users, business stakeholders, product managers and engineers can help teams better understand their users' needs and preferences, helping them create products that are genuinely tailored to the end user. Moreover, an open discovery can also help teams identify any new opportunities or directions that may be worth exploring – potentially providing insight into unique features or services that the competition doesn't offer. When you perform discovery with a multidisciplinary team, chances are that good ideas can originate from any of the participants: an engineer can think about an innovative way to use technology, a business stakeholder can find new untapped markets or a product manager can steer the product towards much better market fit. You get the idea – it's about bringing people together. To conclude, as a UX designer working in the discovery phase of a product, you will have to play two major roles:

- *Own the research efforts:* It is your responsibility to plan, perform and facilitate any user research activities and synthesize findings in an easily digestible form for the entire team to be able to make decisions based on that. This role is about being organized and analytical in your approach so the team can benefit from the most accurate insights possible.
- *Be the bridge that connects ideas and people:* Without performing well in this second role, no amount of good user research findings or eye-catching UI design is going to save your product. This role is about aligning people and ideas, and making sure users are at the core of anything you and your team design.

Continuous discovery

Next, I want to talk about continuous discovery. Ok, what's that now? Let's say we've done an excellent job, went through a successful MVP phase and launched a good product that is starting to have good adoption. Do we just stop there? Of course not; the product still needs to be developed further. Perhaps it needs to work for a different market, or perhaps there is a new feature that can increase adoption. We cannot do that without continuous discovery, particularly after we've launched a product. What you need to remember is 'Product teams make decisions every day. Our goal with continuous discovery is to infuse those daily decisions with as much customer input as possible.'[2] So, what are we basically doing by using continuous discovery? Two things I would say:

- We create a cycle of innovation.
- We de-risk our product decisions through cycles of user research.

Continuous discovery is a critical part of product development after successfully launching a product, its main benefit being the ability to make almost real-time adjustments based on customer feedback or market changes. This provides product organizations with the flexibility they need to be competitive in an ever-evolving market. Continuous discovery is also used to inform the development process, allowing engineering teams to pivot quickly and avoid costly mistakes or delays due to misaligned expectations. Continuous discovery is both a safety net and a magic box of ideas.

Now, you might say, 'Ok, what if I'm not doing continuous discovery? Maybe my team has a very good idea of what we need to build, and we don't need it!' Well, not taking continuous discovery seriously – by going directly into interface design or, even worse, into development without properly gathering precious user insights – can lead to a host of problems. Failing to do continuous discovery in a constant manner means that you risk building something that your users don't actually want or need anymore, resulting in wasted resources and massive frustration for all involved parties. Remember, things change. The research you did one year ago might be invalidated by new market conditions or an aggressive competitor. Why take the chance?

Target painting

Another topic I wanted to touch upon is target painting, also referred to as painting the target around the arrow, or the Texas sharpshooter fallacy, which is, simply put, a logical fallacy that we encounter when dealing with large datasets. This concept originated from epidemiology, where some scientists had the bad practice of drawing conclusions long after certain events took place by using arbitrarily chosen parts of the dataset that would confirm their hypotheses. The name actually comes from the story of a Texan sharpshooter who, in wanting to impress his neighbours, shot randomly at a barn, then proceeded in painting targets where the bullet holes were located. This, of course, impressed his audience and he was declared the best sharp-shooter in the state, but only because they were unaware of the actual chain of events as they happened and took the targets as absolute evidence of his mastery. For you, the learning here is simple: avoid getting too attached to a hypothesis just because some of the data is pointing into that direction.

This is one of the challenges you're going to have with any discovery process (but the concept is not limited to that). What often happens in many of these sessions is that instead of propos-ing solutions for a defined user problem, the group tries to find evidence (usually in the form of user research data) that points to a specific solution they were already contemplating. 'We must go with this solution because user A said they need that feature.' As a UX designer, you will need to be very careful not to fall into this trap yourself when designing and also help the team steer away from doing it, which sometimes might be particularly diffi-cult when you have senior stakeholders that are very opinionated but don't have experience building products. So what should you do in this instance? I would say the answer to this question is always: *go back to the basics*, and help the team create a meaningful and actionable problem statement.[3] One quick way to do that is by reframing the problem. On top of that, make sure you always sense check your work and make sure *you* are not the Texas sharpshooter yourself. It can happen.

Reframing problems can be done through a design thinking lens. This is essential to creating successful products. Starting from the problem space and defining the issue you're trying to solve will help you and your team understand 'the why' behind a product's existence. Discovery helps to uncover opportunities and create clear objectives, which in return drives innovation. Discovery can also provide invaluable insights that help teams make informed decisions when later designing and building products. It helps provide clarity on what problem the team is trying to solve and sets up teams for success in the later stages by ensuring they're working together towards a common goal.

Design thinking

'Ok, what's this design thinking thing you keep telling me about?' I'm glad you asked! Essentially, design thinking is a 'methodology for creative problem-solving'.[4] So what does that mean? Design thinking provides a framework for when you have to solve a problem that is not easy to define. If you cannot define the problem you want to solve, how can you come up with a valid solution?

Similarly to how UX has developed over the years, design thinking has not been born through the efforts of one single individual. Many people contributed to the development of this framework. It started to take shape in the 1970s when people like Horst Rittel, a design theorist and university professor, came up with the concept of wicked problems – problems that are highly complex, ambiguous and have open-ended potential solutions. As this perfectly describes the landscape of building digital products, it is no surprise that this framework gained strong traction in the digital space. The term 'design thinking' was later coined by David Kelley and Tim Brown of IDEO, a design and consulting firm, who pioneered the evolution of this framework to what it is today. A significant contribution also came from Stanford University, particularly from Larry Leifer, a professor of mechanical engineering that researched and introduced engineering design thinking. Design thinking has not stopped evolving. At present, many organizations are using this framework for anything from designing digital products to developing advanced socio-political systems, so there are clear signs that the framework is becoming more and more sophisticated.

As we discussed before, in many instances you will find yourself in a position where stakeholders already have a solution in mind, even before you've formed any problem statement. Or in some cases, user research seems to be pointing in a completely different direction from that of the business team. At other times, people are just confused with the information at hand, which might seem contradictory. In any case, you get the picture. The team is misaligned on a fundamental thing: what is the problem we're trying to solve? This, of course, is a recipe for disaster, as you can imagine, because what happens in reality is that some-one eventually makes a decision and may unilaterally choose a direction for the product. That direction will often end up being the wrong one because we've now compromised user-centricity as a result of misalignment.

So what's all this got to do with design thinking and UX? Because design thinking is a problem-solving framework, using it leads to alignment. So, not only do you get to define your problem in a user-centric way, ideate on solutions and validate those ideas, but you also do it in a way that makes the entire team part of that decision-making process. This creates cohesion in terms of the product vision and aligns the team.

Given all this, it is no surprise that design thinking gained popularity in developing digital products. Particularly valuable in the discovery phase, this framework can help product teams reach a consensus and hit the sweet spot in terms of defining a product's requirements. Design thinking does this at the inter-section of three main dimensions: humans, business and technology (Figure 5.3).

So how does it work? Let's start with the three domains:

- *Humans:* Refers to the human side of a product, mainly its users. It's about gathering information about user needs and goals. Naturally, this is being put into practice through various user research methods.
- *Business:* Refers to the product-level decision-makers and stakeholders that are involved in the product development process and that are responsible for feeding in business

FIGURE 5.3 Design thinking applied to product design

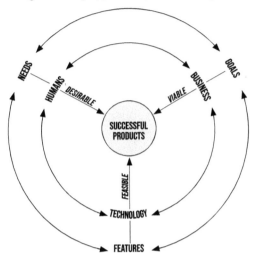

requirements as well as managing the overall business strategy. These stakeholders don't necessarily come from just the business but can also be members of the product team (product managers, UX designers, engineers, etc.).

- *Technology:* Refers mainly to the engineering teams (resourcing, capacity, skills) but also to technology as a whole (complexity, adoption, cost of implementation, etc.).

This framework will allow you to be able to assess a solution from the point of view of these three dimensions. To do so, we need to measure and validate through three lenses:

- *Desirability (humans):* Is the solution satisfying actual user needs? Do users need this solution?
- *Viability (business):* Will the solution fit our business model? Is the solution going to contribute to the sustainability of the

business? Does this solution (even if desired by users) present any risk to the business?

- *Feasibility (technology):* Is the solution technically feasible?

At the intersection of these three dimensions, once everything is validated through the three lenses I've mentioned, is true product innovation.

We've looked at design thinking from a high-level, but how does it actually work in practice? At its core, design thinking involves a five-step process: empathize, define, ideate, prototype and test. The NN/g version of design thinking also adds a sixth step: implement, and I'll explain why this one is also very important. But let's look at each of these steps in more detail (Figure 5.4):

1 *Empathize (or: do your research).* This requires designers to try to understand who their audience is in order to define a

FIGURE 5.4 The six steps of design thinking

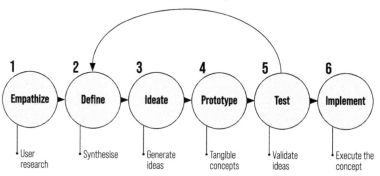

target user. We then extract insights about their needs, goals and expressed feelings through user research. This part of the process is especially important as it helps uncover the 'needs' (areas of opportunity in new products) or 'pain points' (areas where design could be improved if we're talking about an existing product). On top of that, by using design thinking or other ideation frameworks, we can zoom out – we can look at the bigger picture and consider the design problem from a holistic perspective (users, business and technology).

Charles and Ray Eames (two famous industrial designers that revolutionized the American furniture industry in the 1950s) summarized this in a brilliant way: 'Recognizing the need is the primary condition for design.'[5] Without understanding the needs of the users, everything that comes after is just a game of chance. Yes, sometimes you might get lucky and design something that does end up having some product market fit, but in most cases it won't, and the product will fail.

2 *Define (or: synthesise your research).* This helps UX designers turn the insights they've acquired in the empathize phase into a format that can be used for decision making. The define step is basically the process of taking information from multiple research sources (user interviews, stakeholder interviews, analytics, etc.) and combining it to derive a meaningful overall result. Synthesis involves summarizing, evaluating and combining the different sources in order to uncover trends, patterns and themes that can guide design decisions towards successful outcomes. It's a critical piece of the design process for any successful project! As Charles Kettering (who was head of research at General Motors) said: 'A problem well stated is a problem half-solved.'[6] This is the critical moment when your team connects all the dots to make informed decisions.

From this point onwards, design thinking focuses on creative problem-solving rather than simply presenting design solutions based on design best practices or standards.

3 *Ideate (or: generate ideas).* This is when you let yourself and your team go wild! The objective of ideation is twofold: to generate ideas that solve real user needs and are practical, and that are also creative and novel. I know this might sound contradictory, but in practice it's not. Let me explain. The focus during this step is to generate as many ideas as possible without necessarily being limited by functional considerations. Bringing together a multidisciplinary team at this point in time is key. This step ideally involves individuals with diverse perspectives and encourages an open exchange of ideas.

It's important to keep a positive and inclusive mindset during this stage and to avoid the premature filtering of concepts. The goal is to encourage a free flow of ideas, so that the most promising ones can be further developed in the next stage of the design thinking process.

Ask everyone in the team to come up with a variety of possible solutions to the problem or user need identified earlier in the define phase, and then encourage them to share these ideas with one another. This will allow team members to build on top of each other's ideas and re-mix – and this is where the magic usually happens.

4 *Prototype (or: design, refine, repeat).* This is where the rubber meets the road. This is the stage where you take some of those wild and crazy ideas from the previous ideation stage and start turning them into tangible prototypes. During this stage, you can use a variety of materials and tools to give life to your designs, from paper and cardboard to cutting-edge interactive prototypes. The goal is to create something that accurately represents your idea and allows you to test it in a real-world setting. However, sometimes designers tend to miscalculate the level of detail (also called fidelity) needed for testing an idea. Remember? It's ideas we're testing at this stage! In Chapter 7 I will be expanding on this topic and explain what level of fidelity you need to choose when. But, until then, you have to understand one thing: spending lots of time on your

prototypes to compensate for a poor idea will not make your product better. The goal here is to validate ideas as fast as possible. Spend more time refining and iterating than prototyping one single idea. I'm going to conclude with the words of Tom Kelly, author and partner at IDEO: 'If a picture is worth a thousand words, a prototype is worth a thousand meetings.'[7]

5 *Test (or: validate it)*. This is the point in the process when UX designers are able to turn ideas into tangible products for users to interact with and give feedback on. Not only do prototypes help UX designers better understand user needs, but they also provide an excellent way for UX teams to communicate their ideas to other stakeholders involved in the product. With a prototype, UX designers can easily show off their design decisions early and gain instant feedback from both users and stakeholders.

The test phase in design thinking is where the real magic happens! It's the moment of truth you've been waiting for, where you get to see how your ideas hold up in the real world. This is the stage where you get to put them to the test and see how they perform. Think of it as a sports show, where your prototypes are the contestants and the real world is the obstacle course. It's your chance to see if your ideas have what it takes to solve the problem at hand.

During this stage, you'll also be gathering data and feedback from real users, when testing your prototypes in real-world scenarios and observing how they perform. You'll be looking for insights that can help you refine your ideas or discard them in case feedback is negative.

6 *Implement (or: execute the concept)*. This is the extra step that NN/g added in comparison to IDEO or the Stanford versions of this framework.

The implement phase in design thinking is where your ideas finally come to life! This is the stage where you take all the hard work, testing and refining from the previous stages and turn your prototypes into real-world products. Think of it as the grand finale of a fireworks show. All the planning, designing and testing was just the warm-up act, and now it's time for the main event. What would a fireworks show look like without the fireworks? Not very impressive, is it? Being able to execute the vision and put everything you've learned in the previous stages into practice is the most important thing of all.

Design thinking is a powerful and versatile approach to problem-solving that makes use of empathy, experimentation and iteration. It encourages us to look at problems from beyond our individual view to tap into different perspectives and to come up with creative solutions that meet the needs of the users.

Design thinking has proven to be effective in a wide range of contexts, from product design and engineering to business strategy and organizational change. It can help organizations develop new products and services, improve existing ones and find solutions to complex problems. By embracing the principles of design thinking, organizations can create a culture of innovation that allows them to remain competitive and responsive to the changing needs of their customers. Whether you are an aspiring UX designer, entrepreneur, a manager or simply someone who is interested in solving problems in a more effective and human-centred way, design thinking is an approach that is well worth exploring.

Last but not least, design thinking is just one of many problem solving frameworks that exist in the industry. I've only chosen to present this one because of its popularity, but there are also other widely-used frameworks available like the CIRCLES method,[8] root cause analysis, SQUID (sequential question and insight diagram), six sigma model, the Fishbone diagram and many others. On this particular topic I would say *any framework is better than no framework at all*. Frameworks offer the foundations for stakeholder alignment. Following a process offers clarity and you'll end up with a superior product or service. Trust me on this and you'll thank me later.

From user interviews to user story mapping, and everything in between

In this section I want to share my experiences with some of the most popular methods and techniques used in the research and discovery phases. You will encounter these quite frequently during your career, so it's worth studying them more closely. My goal here is not to teach you in-depth how to perform each of these methods but rather to give you some valuable insights and tips that can later help you excel at them. These are based on my learning and personal experience, so context is key.

User research interviews: Are you listening?

We've already covered the basics of this topic, so I'm not going to bore you with the technical details – the type of interview, the context, the set-up and the way you'll analyse the data. But that aside, user research interviews are about only one thing: listening. You may think that you're already doing that, but are you? To listen effectively you need to ensure that you're not talking, you're not interrupting the user's train of thought and you're not interjecting or using leading questions and language. So again, *are you listening?*

I remember watching a film a while ago where one of the protagonists, a detective, was teaching his colleague the art of interviewing, and I'm paraphrasing: 'Every new question is an end to a story.' This is also true for user research. Wearing the hat of a UX researcher, you will have to become very good at listening to your users. That means knowing when and how to keep the conversation flowing, or when to pause if it goes in the wrong direction. I think back to research sessions I've facilitated during my career; perhaps some of the best pieces of insight I've got were when I let the discussion flow without interrupting the interviewee, even though it might have seemed that the conversation was going nowhere. Knowing when to keep listening and communicating using gestures and visual cues and when to intervene is an art you will get better at with time. Just think about this like a game of Tetris; the more you play it, the better you get at fitting the pieces together.

User research interviews: Interpreting data

When performing user research, I would say more than half of the effort will go into interpreting the data you've captured and creating a synthesis. If facilitating interviews can be difficult, trying to find valuable insights in qualitative data can also be a real challenge. Interpreting user research data is a critical part of UX research. It's the process of making sense of the information collected from users through interviews to inform or improve the design of products and services. This is particularly important because, if done wrong, it can essentially invalidate all the effort you've put into the research. This can happen by drawing the wrong conclusions or focusing on the wrong patterns.

But how do UX designers go about analysing interview data to uncover valuable insights? It's important to use the right techniques and tools to make sense of it all. For qualitative data, coding and thematic analysis can be used to identify themes and patterns in the data.

Coding

Coding (not to be misinterpreted as programming) is an essential part of qualitative data analysis that involves classifying and categorizing information according to predetermined criteria. Just to clarify, this is not coding as in 'programming' but a special data analysis technique that helps us tag data by assigning a

FIGURE 5.5 Example of captured user research data showing both coding and thematic analysis (presented in Airtable)

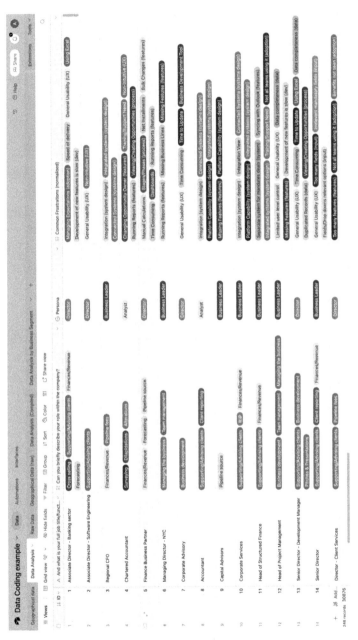

descriptive label to certain data-points with the goal of extracting advanced insights. This process enables researchers to identify patterns, themes and correlations within their data. Coding can be applied to both qualitative and quantitative data and provides an invaluable starting point for further exploration. The first step is to identify the categories into which the information should be organized. These categories can be based on the research objectives or questions asked in the interview. Alternatively, it may also be possible to create them from the data itself by looking closely at specific variables or features.

Once the categories are determined, you can begin tagging the relevant information according to each one. This can involve highlighting text in documents, assigning tags in a digital database, or writing down observations on paper. This will allow you, later, to quickly scan the data to identify trends and patterns.

Thematic analysis

Thematic analysis is a method of interpreting user research data by identifying and exploring patterns and themes. This approach is also commonly used in qualitative research as it allows researchers to gain deeper insights into the data by looking for implicit or hidden meanings within it. To get started with thematic analysis, the first step is to read through the data and gain an understanding of it before grouping similar information together and labelling each group with a descriptive name. These names are typically based on common terms that the participants use to describe their experiences. Then, once all of the themes have been identified, they need to be analysed in depth. This involves looking for relationships between them, and common patterns, as well as exploring any contextual factors that may be influencing these patterns.

While there are many benefits associated with using this method of data interpretation, there are also some limitations to consider, such as time constraints and difficulty in ensuring objectivity when analysing qualitative data sets. Despite these limitations, though, thematic analysis remains a powerful tool for gaining meaningful insights into user behaviour that can help inform product design decisions.

The art of surveys

Surveys are a reliable method for gathering user experience data. For UX, surveys provide vital insights into how people perceive and interact with products and services. In order to create surveys that deliver truly valuable insights, it's essential to understand some tips and tricks behind crafting surveys that give you actionable data.

Using surveys as opposed to user research interviews, for example, has four main advantages that I would like you to remember:

- They allow for large amounts of data collection from a variety of users. This is an important distinction when compared to user research interviews that cannot scale at the same rate.
- They can be used to collect both qualitative and quantitative data so you can get a wide range of perspectives on an issue.
- They are relatively easy to create and administer, allowing you to get valuable insights quicker.
- They open the way to data analysis.

Conducting a survey is not as simple as just throwing a bunch of questions out there and hoping for the best. There is an art to designing effective surveys that deliver accurate and actionable results. To create a successful survey, you must first decide on your research goals and objectives. Are you trying to assess user satisfaction with your current product offerings? Are you looking to gather feedback on a new feature before its release? Are you looking for insights into target users for a new, upcoming product? Understanding your research objectives will help you determine the right type of questions to ask.

Once you have your research goals in place, it's time to start thinking about your survey structure. A well-structured survey should have a clear and concise introduction that sets the tone and explains the purpose of the survey. Don't try to save any effort here. It's crucial that you engage with people from the first second they see the survey; otherwise, they might not answer your questions or, even worse, create an artificial segmentation that will give you inaccurate results later.

Here are a couple of examples:

A POORLY WRITTEN SURVEY INTRO

Welcome to our survey on internet browsers! We are interested in learning about your internet browsing habits and the factors that influence your decisions to use one over the other. To help us better understand your preferences, we would like to ask you a few questions about your income and gender.

This type of introduction could create an artificial segmentation of the participants based on their income or gender, even if that is not really a relevant or meaningful factor in determining their choice of internet browser. It can also create unintended consequences because some people might not want to reveal those details in this context, but they would have been perfectly happy to answer more relevant questions about browsing the internet or their favourite browser.

I would recommend using a neutral and clear introduction that explains the purpose of the survey and the expected length of time it will take to complete. For example:

A WELL-WRITTEN SURVEY INTRO

Thank you for taking the time to participate in this survey. The purpose is to gather information about internet browsers. The survey will take approximately three minutes to complete, and all of your responses will be kept confidential. Your participation is greatly appreciated and will help us to better understand the decision-making process behind choosing your favourite browser.

This second example is clearer, more neutral and sets the tone for the rest of the survey. It also expresses appreciation for the participant's time and emphasizes the importance of their input, increasing the chances of better response rates.

All of these guidelines apply to the actual questions as well. Each of them should be easy to understand and unambiguous, with clear instructions on how to answer. Additionally, the order in which you ask questions can significantly impact the results of your survey, so be mindful of the flow and logic of your questions. You must also decide whether to use qualitative or quantitative data in your survey. Qualitative data focuses on understanding the underlying motivations and attitudes behind user behaviour, while quantitative data provides numerical data that can be easily analysed. Both types of data have their own unique advantages and disadvantages, so the type you choose will depend on your research objectives and the questions you want to answer. Perhaps the best surveys I've ever seen are a mixture of both.

Top tips for crafting effective surveys:

- Choose the right survey type based on your research goals. Surveys can use open or closed questions and should be tailored to the types of data you are looking to collect.
- Keep surveys short and sweet. Surveys with too many questions can overwhelm users and reduce response rates.
- Create surveys that ask about user experience rather than opinions. This will give you more actionable insights into how people are using a product or service.
- Ask straightforward, concise questions with options that make sense. Avoid overly complicated wording as it may confuse respondents.

• Give respondents enough time to complete surveys, but don't let surveys linger for too long. Good surveys should take no more than five minutes to complete.

Once surveys have been administered, it's time to analyse the data. This can be done with a variety of tools, depending on the type and amount of data you have collected. For qualitative questions, you may want to use text analysis software that can help you identify patterns and themes in responses. For quantitative questions, statistical software can be used to analyse trends and correlations in responses.

No matter what kind of survey you create, they are an invaluable tool for gathering user experience data. By following the tips and tricks I've presented here, you can create surveys that get results and provide actionable insight into how your users are interacting with your product.

Personas

Personas are a valuable part of user research and discovery. Personas are created mainly based on user research data. You need to gather all the information you have about your users and segment them based on certain criteria like common needs and goals, or the specific roles they will play within your product. On top of this, you will need to add other elements that help describe these groups of people, sometimes including demographics data, pain-points, psychological traits or usage patterns. In a sense, they are like movie posters: they summarize a lot of information in just one page in an easily digestible format. Personas are representations of real people – aggregated from user research data – that allow us to better understand our target audience. Personas provide a clear character with which we can empathize, allowing us to make decisions that directly benefit the user experience we're creating.

FIGURE 5.6 Example of a user persona

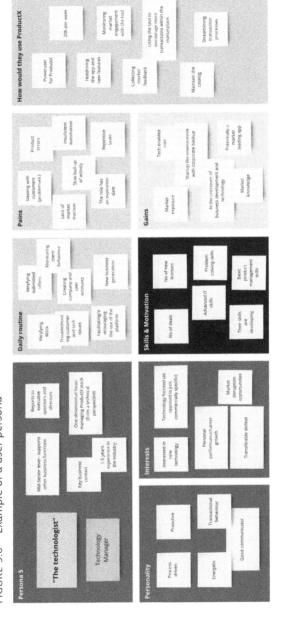

I personally view personas as a good tool for communication rather than an accurate research model; they're there to help teams align and quickly identify user needs and opinions in order to create the best possible product or service. Personas help teams stay focused on the user's needs throughout the design process. Additionally, personas make it easier to align stakeholders around a common goal by giving everyone an idea of who they're designing for. As a result, by understanding how users think, feel and behave, teams can craft solutions that meet their requirements.

Despite their usefulness, there are some limitations associated with personas. Personas can be limited to a single context or product. They often rely on generalizations, which don't always represent individual users accurately. Furthermore, personas are not always based on data gathered from actual users – they may also contain assumptions and opinions coming from designers or product managers. Overall, I would say they are not entirely reliable tools for research, so use them wisely.

Finally, personas are prone to introduce bias in the conversation, and that can translate into designs that don't actually work for the target users. It's a common UX approach to give personas names and faces. While this may seem harmless enough, this practice can have damaging consequences. Let's take a closer look. If you create user personas containing identifying features such as names, photos, or even gender, you will tend to make assumptions about their behaviour based on your own personal experiences. This can lead you and your team to make product decisions based on unreliable data (a mixture of research data and your own opinions/views), viewing the research data through the lens of one individual – you. This will ultimately lead to decisions with potentially serious implications for the success of your product.

So how can we solve this problem? You've already made the first step: you now know you can accidentally introduce bias, so next time you design a user persona, you can try to avoid that as much as possible. My personal approach is not to use names at all, or use something closer to an archetype (e.g. The Explorer, The Patient, The Warehouse Operator, etc.), or if you still want to use a name for sake of more accessible communication, use gender-neutral names (e.g. Jessie, Charlie, Kai, etc.). You could also avoid using images, or use abstract illustrations instead.

As you see, with a few simple precautions, you can make sure that your user personas are still accurate but unbiased – giving you the best chance of creating an accessible and successful product for everyone.

User journeys

The key to a successful product lies in understanding the needs and preferences of its users. User journeys offer an effective way to map these details, making them an essential tool, particularly in the discovery phase of a product. User journeys are essentially stories that map out how users move through your product, from an initial point of contact all the way to the end of the journey and hope to be repeated (for loyal users). To create a user journey, designers must capture their user's motivations and goals while considering how they will interact with each touch point of the user experience (phone, website, app, in person, etc.).

The best metaphor I can think of for user journeys is that of a road trip. Just as a road trip requires careful planning and consideration of the best route with all the stops on the way to successfully reach your destination, a user journey requires the mapping out of the optimal path to help users reach their desired outcome when using a product. By understanding the journey a user takes when using your product, you can identify potential pain points, roadblocks, and areas where the user experience could be improved.

From my personal experience, if there is one thing that significantly elevates the value of this type of artefact, it's the focus on

the *pain points of your users*. A pain point is a problem or difficulty that the user experiences during their journey that hinders
their ability to achieve their goals. These are particularly important when doing discovery for a new product or feature because
fixing them will instantly create a better user experience. These
can be anything from confusing navigation, slow load times, or
a lack of clear instructions. Focusing on pain points is critical
because they are the areas where users are most likely to drop
off or become frustrated with your product (in the case of an
existing product) or areas where they are currently experiencing
frustrations and are on the look out for solutions (new products
or features). By identifying and addressing these pain points and
mapping them against the user journey, you can improve the
overall user experience and make the journey more seamless and
enjoyable. A great example I always give is a confusing checkout
process. It doesn't matter if your UX has been stellar to that
point; if the user drops out at checkout, the entire user experience is ruined. You have a great opportunity to redesign the
process to make it more intuitive and streamline the steps.

My advice when building a user journey is to focus on pain
points and use them as a guide to inform design and development decisions. In this way you can create a user experience that
is optimized for the needs of your target audience. This can lead
to increased engagement, better retention and, ultimately, better
business outcomes.

User story mapping

I've mentioned story mapping before in this book. Story mapping
is the step where you transition from conceptual to concrete. It's
the essential step you need to take between discovery and delivery in order to inform your future backlog. Because this is such
an important step in product development, I want to stress the
fact that it's not just about crafting user stories and dumping
them into a swim lane. It's more about creating order in the

chaos, bringing together high-level insights from your users, combining those with business goals and aligning teams around one vision of what needs to get built. User story mapping will help you make sure everyone is on the same page before diving into full delivery mode (Figure 5.8).

Finally, here are my top tips and tricks when it comes to user story mapping:

- Put together a quick first draft. What I mean by this is, don't spend days in a row crafting the perfect user story statements and trying to organize them, as you will waste lots of time. A quick high-level draft will allow you to start grouping user stories under main themes (usually linked to the user journeys of your personas). Do this first, and make sure you have a solid structure, thinking about where you will start development, what order you want to tackle them in and so on. Leave refinement to the very end.
- If you are lucky enough (as I was on many occasions) to work with brilliant product managers and engineers, make sure they are part of this step. This is not a job for UX *or* product management *or* engineering. This is a job for the entire team. This is not negotiable if you want a successful product down the line.
- Once you have a decent version of it, put it in front of your business stakeholders and validate again that everyone is aligned.
- Prioritize! This a fantastic chance to start prioritizing your future backlog because you have a nice aerial view of the product and its features. Once this gets into Jira (a popular project management tool), it's not going to be as easy to have the same conversations.

Your user is not the product owner!

I've touched on this point earlier in this book, but the time has come to dive into this topic because it's absolutely critical for

FIGURE 5.7   Example of a simple user journey map

Persona: Customer service representation
Scenario and scope: A ProductX CSR receives a request that requests
the creation of a ticket in the system

	STEP 1 Identify caller information and details	STEP 2 Understand and code/ classify type of work	STEP 3 Create ticket and approval chain
User actions	Use ProductX (Alpha integration) to identify the caller. Log into the given Client account Verify the caller's identity and location for the request.	Understand all the details about the client's problem. Ask clarifying questions to get assess the issue. Choose the ticket code and extra details.	Assigns ticket to service provider. Confirms priority and response time from provider. Creates approval chain. Submits ticket.
Pain points and opportunities	The user has to access each client account with long load times. Some corporate clients, have multiple accounts: for admin, retail, finances etc CSRs can get locked out when the data is being updated. When creating a new caller ticket, CSR is forced to fill in some fields that are unknown.	Assigning a ticket code can be an abstract and difficult task. Each Client account has its customised list of ticket codes. There is no centralized list of clarifying questions. Selecting a ticket code, wipes out the problem description if it was filled in before.	Very small area for entering ticket comments. Extra steps required to select the right approval chain with the right level of hierarchy.
User experience			

| **Tools and resources used** | Using ProductX for logging in into the client account.

Using Excel to track the daily timesheet.

Using Outlook for internal and external communications.

Using Google Maps to identify the client location.

Using third party identity verification service. | Using ProductX for creating the ticket and details.

Using Excel to track the daily timesheet.

Using Outlook for internal and external communications. | Using ProductX for creating the ticket and details.

Using Excel to track the daily timesheet.

Using Outlook for internal and external communications.

Using Track-360 for managing ticket lifecycle |

STEP 4 Get sign-off from relevant parties	STEP 5 Send any additional requests to service provider	STEP 6 Verbal Hand-off with the Service Provider
Get insurance sign-off. Get line management sign-off. Submits approval.	Send any additional requests manually to the service provider. Escalate with Service Manager as and when required.	Verbal hand-off with the chosen service provider. Escalate with Service Manager as and when required.
Getting sign-off is often a painful manual process. Sometimes insurers don't respond to requests in a timely manner. Each Client account has its customized list of approval codes. The user has to use multiple systems that are not connected to each other to do this.	Sending additional requests is a very painful process sometimes because service providers need various details that the CSR does not have at hand. The process is very time-consuming and frustrating taking much longer than all the other work.	Needs to manually copy and paste data like phone numbers, addresses from ProductX into their system – with many of these in various non-standard formats. Unfriendly ticket tracking system. Difficult to escalate when Service Managers are on annual leave and the escalation tree is often broken.

| Using ProductX for creating the ticket and details. Using Excel to track the daily timesheet. Using Outlook for internal and external communications. Phone calls. | Using ProductX for creating the ticket and details. Using Excel to track the daily timesheet. Using Outlook for internal and external communications. Phone calls. | Using ProductX for creating the ticket and details. Using Outlook for internal and external communications. Phone calls. |

FIGURE 5.8 Example of user story mapping

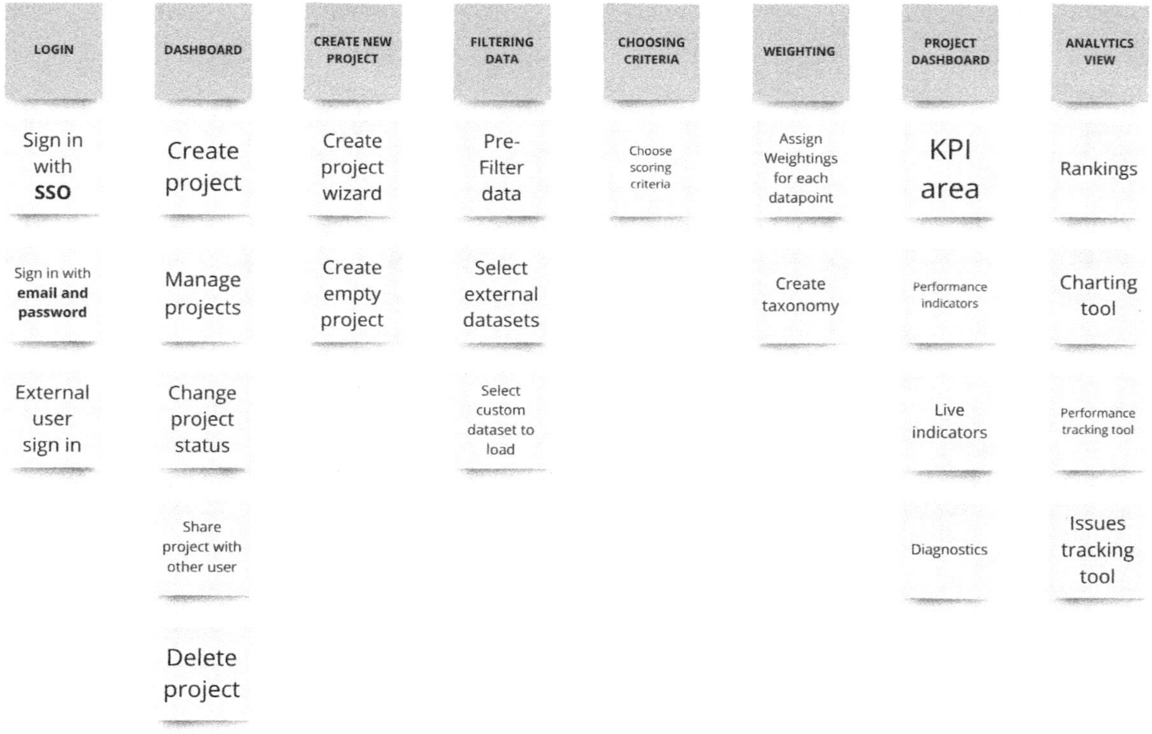

LOGIN	DASHBOARD	CREATE NEW PROJECT	FILTERING DATA	CHOOSING CRITERIA	WEIGHTING	PROJECT DASHBOARD	ANALYTICS VIEW
Sign in with **SSO**	Create project	Create project wizard	Pre-Filter data	Choose scoring criteria	Assign Weightings for each datapoint	KPI area	Rankings
Sign in with **email and password**	Manage projects	Create empty project	Select external datasets		Create taxonomy	Performance indicators	Charting tool
External user sign in	Change project status		Select custom dataset to load			Live indicators	Performance tracking tool
	Share project with other user					Diagnostics	Issues tracking tool
	Delete project						

you to understand it perfectly, no matter if you're an aspiring designer, product manager, engineer or entrepreneur.

We've all heard the phrase, 'The customer is always right.' But when it comes to product design and UX, our user isn't always 'right'. In fact, they often don't know what they need or want until we give them a product that meets those needs. As Jakob Nielsen, co-founder of NN/g, said: 'To design the best UX, pay attention to what users do, not what they say. Self-reported claims are unreliable, as are user speculations about future behaviour. Users do not know what they want.'[9]

First of all, let's set the scene right and define the variables. When we talk about user 'needs', we're referring to what they actually require in order to complete their goal. For example, if you're building a mobile application for a local restaurant, the user's needs might include the ability to see a menu, place an order and pay for their food online. These are the bare minimum requirements for the product to be useful. On the other hand, a user's 'wants' are more aspirational – they're the things that they would like to have, from their viewpoint as individuals, thus they are less essential for the actual product as a whole. For example, some users might want the application to include a table reservation feature because they want their favourite table with a view of the city; others might want a rewards feature because they eat there frequently; while others would like to be able to access detailed nutritional information for each dish. These are nice to have, but they're not what the average user actually needs in order to use the application effectively. The problem with an approach like this is that it ignores the bigger picture – it ignores the users as a whole. Just because 'a user' is asking for a particular feature, it doesn't mean it's the right thing for the product as a whole. What often happens is that users ask for features that are technically not feasible or would take a long time to implement and would distract from other, more important parts of the product.

The product team is responsible for determining the product vision and features backlog based on user needs, market trends and business goals. They're also responsible for prioritizing features accordingly. This means that while user feedback should always be taken into consideration, we shouldn't hand over the control of the product vision – otherwise, product owners run the risk of being pulled in different directions by user 'wants' instead of focusing on what's best for the product holistically.

Of course, this doesn't mean the user's 'wants' and feedback should be completely ignored. Far from it! The user is a vital source of information that can help the product team make informed decisions about what to build. But at the end of the day, the team needs to make the final call about what's best for the product and the business.

Remember, the user is not the product owner!

Notes

1   Interaction Design Foundation (2023) What is UX research? Interaction Design
    Foundation, nd. www.interaction-design.org/literature/topics/ux-research
    (archived at https://perma.cc/3WXN-7KS8)

2   T Torres (2021) *Continuous Discovery Habits: Discover products that create
    customer value and business value*, Product Talk LLC, Portland, Oregon

3   R Friis Dam and T Yu Siang. Stage 2 in the design thinking process: Define the
    problem and interpret the results, Interaction Design Foundation, 22 November
    2019. www.interaction-design.org/literature/article/stage-2-in-the-design-
    thinking-process-define-the-problem-and-interpret-the-results (archived at
    https://perma.cc/HW5T-W83J)

4   Stanford D.School. Get started with design thinking, Stanford D.School, nd.
    dschool.stanford.edu/resources/getting-started-with-design-thinking (archived at
    https://perma.cc/7D67-7WGS)

5   Library of Congress. The work of Charles and Ray Eames: A legacy of
    invention, Library of Congress, nd. www.loc.gov/exhibits/eames/furniture.html
    (archived at https://perma.cc/V4Y5-AM9W)

6   GoodReads. Charles Franklin Kettering: Quotes, GoodReads, nd. www.
    goodreads.com/quotes/449969-a-problem-well-stated-is-a-problem-half-solved
    (archived at https://perma.cc/V2AS-LP3F)

7   B Boyle. Learn more before you invest more, IDEO U, nd. www.ideou.com/
    blogs/inspiration/learn-more-before-you-invest-more (archived at https://perma.
    cc/7E4V-NFCS)

8   L C Lin (2019) *Decode and Conquer*, 3rd edn, Impact Interview, Seattle, WA

9   J Nielsen. First rule of usability? Don't listen to users, NN/g, 4 August 2001.
    www.nngroup.com/articles/first-rule-of-usability-dont-listen-to-users (archived
    at https://perma.cc/UJ64-EKA8)

CHAPTER SIX

Data-driven UX

Data, believe it or not, is the lifeblood of UX design. Without data to inform our decisions, UX would be just decoration, and we would need to rely on intuition and personal experience alone to design our interfaces. But with data-driven insights within reach, we can tap into a wealth of information that can shape our decisions. This is why data is becoming central to every UX designer's process: it enables us to confidently craft compelling experiences that meet users' needs and even exceed their expectations! And it doesn't have to be as intimidating as it might seem; in this chapter, I'll try to be your guide to unlocking the power of data-driven user experience design.

The importance of data in UX design

I'm happy to say that data-driven UX design is becoming an increasingly prevalent approach, where design decisions are based on data and user research rather than assumptions or personal opinions. When we use data to drive the design process, we can create more user-centred and compelling experiences that deliver real value to users.

Data, in general, provides invaluable insights into how people use and interact with websites, apps and other digital products. For example, data gathered from user research studies and surveys can be used to identify patterns in users' behaviour, helping designers develop better solutions for their target audience. Data-driven design decisions are also backed up by concrete evidence rather than intuition or guesswork, which makes them more reliable over time. By doing data-driven UX, you can elevate your conversations with stakeholders and deliver evidence-based design decisions.

Next, I would like to provide some examples of areas of UX where data plays a key role.

User research and testing data

Data gathered through user research and usability testing is one of the most important sources of information for UX designers. This data can include information about user behaviours, motivations, pain points and preferences. Essentially, the needs and wants, as I referred to them earlier. As UX designers, we use this data to identify these user needs, validate design decisions and iterate our designs to create better user experiences. This usually comes in the form of unstructured data (words, phrases, etc.). As I explained earlier in this book, this type of data can be pretty tricky to analyse, and it's essential to follow research 'best practices'.

Analytics data

Usually coming in the form of structured data, showing key stats about how users move through the system, user analytics provide us with data on how people are actually interacting with the product, all in a quantified way. Analytics data can include information about user engagement, usage patterns, funnels and drop-off points. You can use this data to identify areas where the user experience can be improved and to measure the effectiveness of any design changes. While analytics data might be easier to understand (as it's easier to visualize structured data in tables and charts, etc.), it's not necessarily easy to interpret. In fact, I would say that, based on my experience, there's a high chance that you will misinterpret your analytics data more than a few times until you get better at it. This type of data is very prone to cause-and-effect relationship fallacies. Nate Silver, a renowned American statistician and TV personality, has a very entertaining way of explaining this in laymen's terms:

> Most of you will have heard the maxim 'correlation does not imply causation.' Just because two variables have a statistical relationship with each other does not mean that one is responsible for the other. For instance, ice cream sales and forest fires are correlated because both occur more often in the summer heat. But there is no reason; you don't light a patch of the Montana brush on fire when you buy a pint of Haagen-Dazs.[1]

So, when talking about analytics data, you will often find yourself trying to find patterns where there aren't any. While this data is one of the most important ones you can lean on as a UX designer, it needs to be treated with the utmost consideration. Any design decision made on the back of a flawed data analysis is bound to affect your product negatively. This is not a prediction but a fact.

A/B testing data

A/B testing is a powerful tool for UX designers that allows them to compare different designs and determine which one performs best. It's a close relative to user research and analytics, largely because it uses lots of the methodology that's being used there too. By gathering data on user engagement, conversion rates, drop-off points, etc., UX designers can make informed decisions about which design elements to keep and which to change.

'Easier said than done,' you'll say. Well, yes, I agree A/B testing data can get tricky, as the best way to interpret is through a combination of qualitative and quantitative data analysis, so examining it and drawing conclusions can be difficult. If I have one piece of advice when it comes to A/B testing, that would be: never rely on just the quantitative aspect of the test to draw conclusions or you risk making some bad decisions.

User demographics data

Data such as age, gender, location, educational background, economic factors, etc., can help UX designers better understand the target audience of the product and create designs that are more relevant to our users. One of the ways to get to know them better is by looking at demographic data. Demographic data helps us get a sense of who our users are, what their high-level characteristics are, and what they might need or expect from our product based on that.

Think of it this way: if you were designing a video game, for example, you would want to know if your target audience is primarily made up of young kids, teens, adults or a combination of these. This information would inform important decisions around the level of difficulty, type of content and overall style of the game. But, as I mentioned before, it's not just about age; demographics can include information such as gender, location, education, finances and more. This data can give us a better understanding of the cultural and societal norms of our users and help us design a product that is not only usable but cultur- ally and socially appropriate.

For example, if you're designing an application for an elder care facility, you'll want to make sure the font is big enough for elderly users who may have vision issues, or if you're designing an app for children, you will have to take into account things like type of content (which needs to be appropriate for their age), safeguarding and a friendly interface. This is where demographic data comes in very handy, allowing us to have that extra layer of information on top of our user research and analytics. One thing I should caution you about is *never to use demographics data in isolation*. While it's very insightful, it cannot be a substitute for user research or usability testing.

Customer feedback data

Customer feedback provides UX designers with valuable insights into what users like and dislike about the product or service. This data is usually gathered through customer support interactions like phone calls, support emails, chats, online reviews or surveys. Data coming from the support or marketing teams of a product can be very helpful in our UX design efforts. However, you need to be mindful of the fact that this is still proxy data. I briefly talked about this in Chapter 1. My advice there still stands – by all means, capture and use this data as a valuable source of information, but in no circumstances should you use it to replace user research data. UX designers can use this data to identify areas for improvement, prioritize design changes and ultimately contribute to creating a more positive user experience.

Predictive analytics

Hopefully, you enjoyed reading some of the predictions I made in Chapter 1 about emerging technologies and their role in the future of UX design. Well, this is another one. With the rise of machine learning and AI, a new generation of UX tools has entered the market. These are predictive analytics tools for UX. They come in many shapes and forms, but the ones I want to talk about the most are those trying to predict the future behaviour of users based on visual designs. So how does this work? Predictive analytics is a technique that uses data, statistical algorithms and machine learning techniques to identify the likelihood of future outcomes based on historical data. In my particular example, this type of tool uses large datasets of eye-tracking data, heat maps, click maps, etc.

So why do I think this technology can be a game changer for UX design? Imagine having the ability to predict wherever a design will perform well in front of users just by using historical data. This can significantly increase the speed at which you, as a designer, can test and validate concepts. Think of a future where you will no longer have to do in-person usability testing, but instead you can use an AI tool, select the user type (demographics, preferences, goals, etc.) and put your designs to the test. See where the user's attention will be, what content they will read first and where your layout performs best.

Sounds exciting, right?. Yes, predictive analytics can be a powerful tool. Yes, when based on large datasets of historical data, predictions can get quite close to the results you would get from usability testing or even analytics. But there is a catch. Predictive analytics can only tell you what would happen based on what has already happened before. That's it. You get a result. It cannot help you to understand why users behave a certain way and how you might expect them to behave in the future. Predictive analytics for UX offers a snapshot into a potential future. Usability testing, on the other hand, is the whole video scene.

That is why UX design will still be here in the future. Even if tools like the one I described just now can help us extract more insights faster, nothing beats the wealth of information you get directly from a user through a user research interview or a usability test. By studying user behaviour, motivations and goals, UX designers can go beyond what AI can do. As designers, we can ask users questions, and we can expand or pivot that conversation and open the way to ideas that were not even considered before. While predictive analytics is a fantastic tool, it should never completely replace core user research techniques, but rather complement them.

Qualitative vs quantitative data

In Chapter 5 we reviewed some of the most important user research methods that we can use as UX designers. We looked at how we can categorize them, and one way of doing that is through the qualitative vs quantitative dimension. So, focusing just on data, what is the difference between these two categories? When it comes to UX design, qualitative and quantitative data each provide valuable information that can be used to inform the design process. Although these two types of data are different from one another, neither is more important than the other. Both qualitative and quantitative research serve different purposes, but they complete each other in helping UX designers create a better user experience for their products or services.

Qualitative data

Qualitative data is often used for gathering insights through interviews and observations into how people interact with a product or service. It is a type of non-numerical data that describes the features or characteristics of things rather than quantities. This type of data is subjective in nature and can reveal important insights about how users feel about the product or service. Qualitative research allows for open-ended conversations with users so researchers can get an authentic understanding of their motivations and feelings.

It's no secret that understanding the user's decision-making process is an integral part of successful user experiences. We want to make sure our users are making choices that best suit their needs and goal, so how can we ensure this by using qualitative data? Enter Daniel Kahneman's concept of System 1 and System 2 thinking. The idea behind it is simple: System 1 is the 'fast thinking' we do automatically, while System 2 requires effortful, thus slower, mental activity. According to Kahneman,

System 1 relies on heuristics (a set of mental shortcuts), while System 2 involves more 'long-form' analytical reasoning.

For example, let's say you're designing the marketing page for a game. In order to encourage sales, you might use a large hero image with a clear call-to-action button and engaging content to motivate users to buy the featured game as soon as possible. As you can imagine, this will be using System 1 thinking: a quick, instinctive decision that can have positive results. You will be effectively planning the user experience by strategizing around System 1 thinking. On the other hand, if you're trying to design an enterprise application for the finance department, this might require a lot more strategizing around System 2 thinking. Given the context, you'll need to put in a lot more effort in to consider the best layout for the screens, the hierarchy of information and which elements should be prioritized and revealed first to the user.

Both forms of thought processes are essential for successful UX design – but understanding when and where each one is useful and in what context is key. System 1 thinking can entice the user to make decisions quickly and instinctively (like a simple A/B test between two colour choices for a button), while System 2 requires analytical reasoning for more complex designs (like asking the user what they feel about the design of a data table). Qualitative data will take centre stage when we plan our future designs. Having data that allows us to understand what users say and infer what their needs are is an invaluable asset for UX designers. However, as you can imagine, it's never as simple as just reading and interpreting qualitative data. Daniel Kahneman makes that clearer in his book, *Thinking, Fast and Slow*:

> Mood evidently affects the operation of System 1: when we are
> uncomfortable and unhappy, we lose touch with our intuition.
> These findings add to the growing evidence that good mood,
> intuition, creativity, gullibility, and increased reliance on System 1
> form a cluster. At the other pole, sadness, vigilance, suspicion, an

analytic approach, and increased effort also go together. A happy mood loosens the control of System 2 over performance: when in a good mood, people become more intuitive and more creative, but also less vigilant and more prone to logical errors.[2]

There are many factors that can contribute to the decision-making process of a user. As UX designers, we need to focus on the ones that we can influence more and understand that even the best strategy can sometimes fail due to the complexity of the human psyche.

Here are my top tips and tricks for when you have to deal with qualitative data:

- *Open-ended questions* are your best friend. These will encourage participants to provide more detailed responses, and you can probe deeper.
- *Be flexible* during your research sessions, allowing participants to take the conversation in unexpected directions. This might not go anywhere but can sometimes offer you some real gems.
- *Recruiting* research participants is as important as the sessions themselves. Use a diverse group of participants to gather a variety of perspectives.
- *Synthesis* is key to understanding qualitative research. Thoroughly analyse the data using a coding framework to identify themes and patterns. Don't just present high-level findings that you might have noted down in your notebook.
- *Use quotes from your users.* This is one of the most powerful tools you can use. Don't shy away from using key quotes in your research reports or stakeholder meetings.

Quantitative data

On the other hand, quantitative data provides useful information on user behaviour patterns, allowing UX designers to understand how users interact with a product or service. In short, quantitative data is numerical data that can be measured and expressed using numbers. This type of data is mainly gathered through analytics, but also other techniques like surveys, A/B testing, card sorting, etc., and it's used to measure certain user behaviours over time. It comes in many shapes or forms, like funnel analysis, usage stats, click-maps, heat maps, survey analysis and many, many more.

Quantitative research allows designers to identify trends in user behaviour and make decisions based on numerical evidence rather than subjective opinion. The advantage of quantitative data is that it's usually faster to collect, analyse and interpret compared to qualitative data. It provides a general overview of user behaviour and preferences, allowing for easy comparison between different user types. However, as you can imagine, quantitative data is quite limited in its ability to provide detailed insights into the user's experience. It cannot single-handedly explain why users behave in a certain way, sometimes making it difficult to identify the root cause of a problem.

And because I know you've been waiting for this, here are my top tips and tricks for quantitative data:

- *Clearly define the research goal* before gathering data. Running research without a goal or a hypothesis is more of an exploratory effort, almost like saying, 'Let's talk to people and just see what happens.' This is not a good idea, and it will almost always lead to inferior results.
- *Make sure you hit statistical significance.* The higher the sample size, the better your analysis will be. Without reaching statistical significance, you run the risk of drawing erroneous conclusions.
- *Mix data collection methods.* Don't limit yourself to just one data source. It's usually a good idea to triangulate your data collection. This can also be applied to qualitative research data.
- *Always visualize your data.* Tables, charts, heat maps, etc., can all open up new ways of looking at the data and can offer you new avenues for insights. Don't be afraid to experiment with visualization. It's also a potent tool for communicating findings with stakeholders.

To conclude, both types of data are necessary for understanding how people perceive and interact with products or services, giving UX designers greater insight into their designs. By combining quantitative data with qualitative data we can gain a deeper understanding of what our users think, feel and do. This allows us to design products or services that better meet the needs of our target users. Quantitative research is an invaluable instrument for UX designers and should be used in conjunction with qualitative research to obtain a well-rounded picture when developing user experiences.

Attitudinal vs behavioural data

Next, I'm going to talk about attitudinal vs behavioural data for UX design. If you remember what we discussed in Chapter 5, this refers to the 'what people do'/what people say' dimension.[3] Attitudinal and behavioural are two fundamental data types that can be used to 'measure' user experiences. Attitudinal data paints a picture of *what users say and feel about an experience*, while behavioural data tells us *what they do in response to that experience*. They both have their advantages and disadvantages, so it's essential to understand the difference between them when using data for designing user experiences.

Attitudinal data

This type of data is usually gathered from surveys or interviews that measure users' opinions and feelings about a product or service. This type of data provides very valuable insight into how people view a user experience, but it often lacks specifics related to individual actions taken by users. As an aspiring UX professional, you know that understanding how users feel about your product is just as important as knowing how they use it. And that's where attitudinal data comes in. This type of data provides insights into users' opinions, attitudes and preferences. It can help you understand what your target users want and need, and how they expect the product or service to work. In a way, it's like having a direct line to the users' brains. Well, almost, because attitudinal data can be subjective and prone to bias.

Without attitudinal data, you would be designing in the dark. You would have difficulties knowing whether users found your product confusing or whether they loved it. You wouldn't know whether they were using it the way it was intended or whether they were finding clever workarounds for completing their tasks. So, attitudinal data can offer a great richness of information that you can use to iterate and improve your user experiences. You can get a sense of what's working and what's not. You can identify areas for improvement and prioritize design decisions based on this user feedback. It allows you to design with empathy instead of making assumptions about your users.

There are, of course, a few advantages to using attitudinal data, like the fact that it can detect subtle changes in feelings, or it can help us to understand why users take specific actions (trying to figure that out just from quantitative or behavioural data, for example, would be an almost impossible task). Finally, using this type of data allows companies to be proactive and address issues before they become too serious.

When talking about disadvantages, I would like to mention the potential bias in respondents' opinions, the small sample sizes that sometimes can make it difficult to identify meaningful conclusions or the simple fact that attitudinal data can be time-consuming to gather and analyse (particularly when running interviews or focus groups).

Behavioural data

Behavioural data provides insights into how users interact with your product or service. This type of data can be collected through user analytics, user testing, A/B testing, or other more niche methods such as eye-tracking. This type of data helps UX designers understand how users navigate through the product, where they encounter problems, and how they use your product or service. Behavioural data can be limited in scope and doesn't always provide insights into the 'why' behind a user's behaviour. It's basically like watching someone perform their tasks, but you won't necessarily have any insights into why they are doing certain things.

In terms of the advantages of using behavioural data, perhaps the most important one is that it offers us concrete evidence of user behaviour and the fact that once we gather historical data (particularly applicable for analytics), we can track changes over time, which is very important for products. The same analytics can also be used in real time, meaning that we can track behavioural changes live. This allows us to identify potential problems with new releases or changes in behavioural patterns that might be triggered by external factors (e.g. a new competitor product launch).

For disadvantages, I would like to mention the difficulty of interpreting this data. I approached this topic earlier in this chapter. Behavioural data can be difficult to interpret, and it's also prone to data analysis abnormalities such as false correlations, as was demonstrated earlier with Nate Silver's example of ice creams and forest fires.

In conclusion, behavioural data is a great asset in a UX designer's toolkit, but you need to be very careful not to draw the wrong conclusions from it.

Sure, attitudinal data can be subjective and biased, and behavioural data can be prone to false correlations, but with the right approach, we can minimize those issues. My advice would be to combine behavioural data with attitudinal data because this can provide a complete picture of the user experience.

Data analysis for UX

Data analysis is an essential step in the process of UX design and research that can make or break a design. As we concluded earlier in this book, in order to create products that people love, it's essential to understand their needs and preferences. To do that, we perform user research using a wide array of methods, techniques and technologies. By gathering data on user behaviour, preferences and pain points, as UX designers, we can create products that meet their specific needs, avoiding any frustrations and building what we call 'delightful experiences'.

But gathering data is only the first step we need to take. It's equally important that once we have gathered the data, we thoroughly analyse that data in a meaningful way. This is where data analysis for UX comes in. By examining the data collected from user research, designers can gain insights into what users need or want from a product. These insights will be used to inform design decisions later.

Analysing data involves understanding data points, interpreting them correctly and using them to inform design decisions. There is no one-size-fits-all approach when it comes to data analysis; successful data analysis requires critical thinking and creativity, as well as a good grasp of analytical tools such as data visualization tools or statistical analysis tools.

Here are my top tips and tricks when it comes to data analysis for UX:

- *Always use a structured approach.* When analysing user research data, it's vital to use a structured approach. This means defining clear research questions, setting specific objectives and creating a plan for how the data will be collected and analysed. Last but not least, this also applies to qualitative data. Remember what we discussed earlier in this chapter in regards to coding qualitative data.
- *Use the right tool for the job.* People tend to discount this aspect a lot. There are a variety of tools available for analysing user research data, from spreadsheets to specialized software. Make sure you're using the right tools for the job. This will massively speed up your work and allow you to

extract better insights. I'll talk more about specific tools in Chapter 12.

- *Try to be objective.* When interpreting data, try to bypass individual opinions. Data analysis should be as unbiased as possible. Of course, it's not always easy to achieve this 100 per cent, but making a conscious effort will always end in better results. Steven Few, in his book *Signal: Understanding what matters in a world of noise*, talks about this very topic: 'To find signals in data, we must learn to reduce the noise – not just the noise that resides in the data, but also the noise that resides in us. It is nearly impossible for noisy minds to perceive anything but noise in data.'[4]
- *Be focused on looking for patterns.* One of the main goals of data analysis is to identify patterns and trends in the data. Look for recurring themes and behaviours to gain insights into what users want and need. Doing this also opens up new opportunities for having strategic-level conversations with stakeholders.
- *Data visualization as a communication tool.* Familiarize yourself with data visualization. That will help you present collected data in an easily understandable format for a wide audience. People tend to digest visuals much better than long-form text content.

Of course, doing data analysis for UX doesn't come without any challenges. One of the most common pitfalls is data overload. Collecting too much data or data that isn't relevant to the product can lead to confusion and impede your ability to make informed decisions. It will also prevent you from being able to efficiently analyse it. It's important to have a clear idea of what data you need before conducting any data collection so as not to become overwhelmed by irrelevant information. Another common issue is data misinterpretation. Data can tell us a lot about how our users interact with our products, but if the data is misread or interpreted incorrectly, it can lead us to make poor design decisions. I've talked about this extensively in the previous sections, but it's worth reinforcing. This is why product managers and UX designers need to have open communication throughout the data analysis process. Data should be critically considered and insights should be validated carefully before being used to inform design decisions.

Finally, if there is one constant in the product word, that is change. User research data can also become outdated quickly, mainly when product updates come out frequently or when we operate in a very dynamic market sector with lots of competitors trying to innovate. Keeping research data up-to-date is crucial in order to ensure that the insights are still valid and useful for creating compelling designs. It's important to develop data collection processes that allow you to easily incorporate new data as your product changes over time.

Data analysis helps us identify and fix any potential design flaws quickly, saving us time and money in the long run. Without data analysis, it would be almost impossible to create meaningful experiences that accurately meet user needs. So, for every aspiring UX designer or product professional out there, data analysis can be your friend! Take the time to synthesize and understand it and use it to inform your decisions and communicate to the team – you won't regret it.

Notes

1   N Silver (2015) *The Signal and the Noise: Why so many predictions fail – but some don't*, Penguin Books, New York
2   D Kahneman (2011) *Thinking, Fast and Slow*, Farrar, Straus and Giroux, New York
3   C Rohrer. When to use which user-experience research methods, NN/g, 17 July 2022. www.nngroup.com/articles/which-ux-research-methods (archived at https://perma.cc/W9LD-UDH8)
4   S Few (2015) *Signal: Understanding What matters in a world of noise*, Analytics Press, Burlingame, California

CHAPTER SEVEN

Interaction design

Interaction design (IxD) is an integral part of UX design. It's essentially the step where user experiences transition from conceptual to concrete. Many non-professionals tend to interpret it as the point in time where our user experiences become visual, but in fact IxD includes many other elements that go beyond just pure aesthetics like sound, motion, content (text), space (if we're talking about a physical experience), etc. The main goal of IxD is to make products intuitive, easy to use, and enjoyable. It is a key element in creating an exceptional user experience and should *always* be informed by thorough user research.

As someone interested in UX design, you might be wondering: what exactly is IxD and how does it fit into the UX discipline? In this chapter I will provide an introduction to this specialty as well as its connection to UX. We'll discuss why IxD is so important and what skills are needed to succeed.

The great debate: UX vs UI

It's not hard to understand why IxD has become a very attractive discipline for UX or product designers – after all, who can resist great visuals? But, as I mentioned just now, it's not about the visuals. In some cases your interface might have limited or even no visual elements (e.g. smart speakers like Echo with its Alexa AI assistant). Does that mean there's no IxD involved? Of course not, it just means the weight of that interface is heavily tilted towards sounds and voice feedback, less on visual cues. As a UX designer it's very important to understand this concept, because it will enable you to design better interfaces when you're looking at your user experience with a holistic view.

Historically, even though UX in theory is an 'older' practice than IxD, it was IxD that took centre stage for a long time, particularly at the beginning of the internet era. Why is that? Well, because everyone can be a designer, right? If you have access to the right tools to produce visuals, and have some native talent in producing aesthetically pleasing designs, you're a designer. And for a long time, that was the norm. Effectively, an entire step in the UX process was skipped for at least a decade. Designers back then were called 'web designers', and would just go directly into designing the UI, usually based on a brief, or even worse, based on some conversations with the business stakeholders. While this in many cases started to produce visually pleasing designs, the user experience was just not there. Everything around user needs, business needs, technology limitations, etc., was merely an afterthought and most UX decisions were made based on assumptions. To state the obvious, this didn't turn out very well. While users can forgive a less appealing UI which gives them exactly what they need, they will never forgive a beautiful UI that just doesn't cater to their goals. Professionals realized that IxD without user research, even with all best practices adhered to, becomes one thing: *decoration*.

Needless to say, there are still echoes of that even today, where less UX mature organizations hire visual/UI designers and just jump right into producing interfaces based on stakeholder input. As you may suspect, that simply doesn't work, and many large-scale organizations are struggling with this aspect. To complicate things even more, some organizations have also split IxD into more specialities, particularly trying to distinguish between an 'interaction designer' and a 'UI designer'. While this level of granularity might give some clarity when it comes to highly specialized individuals, overall it hurts the industry as it creates massive confusion for both aspiring designers and hiring managers that are less experienced with design. I'm going to cover this and a lot more in Chapter 12. For the purpose of this book, I will keep UI and interaction designers under the same IxD umbrella

But, let's focus back on the present! IxD is essentially a part of UX, a step in the whole process, if I may. Remember that non-linear process I was talking about in the beginning of the book? It still applies here. In reality, the process is not linear and we will often loop back while doing continuous discovery. IxD focuses on the interaction between the user and the product, while UX as a whole looks at the bigger picture – how does this interaction fit into the overall product, how do we design it in a way that we meet our user's goals or how do we make that experience delightful? A strong UX designer will have a holistic view of UX principles while also understanding how to design effective user interfaces.

While both UX and IxD are very important in the context of creating user experiences, they do require different sets of skills. And this is where this whole industry-wide debate has its origins. Let's forget for a second that IxD is an integral part of UX, and let's highlight the differences in hard skills that are needed to perform each of them at a professional level. Table 7.1 is by no means an exhaustive list but rather gives you a better idea of what the overlap is.

TABLE 7.1   The skill set and techniques needed for UX design and IxD

Skill Set or Technique	UX Designer	Interaction Designer
User research	Required	Optional
Workshop facilitation	Required	Optional
User journeys	Required	Optional
Task flows	Required	Optional
Information architecture	Required	Required
Wireframing	Required	Required
Visual design	Optional	Required
Prototyping	Required	Required
Usability testing	Required	Optional
User flows	Required	Required
Motion	Optional	Optional
Sound design	Optional	Optional
Spatial design	Optional	Optional

When it comes to soft skills, in my experience both specialities will need similar ones. Perhaps the most important one is empathy, as that drives everything else in your day-to-day job as a UX or interaction designer. Other soft skills that are very important:

- Good communication skills, or the ability to confidently present designs and solutions to a wide audience.
- Collaboration skills, or the ability to work in a multidisciplinary team.
- Time management skills.

- Attention to detail.
- Creativity, or the ability to come up with innovative solutions to given problems.
- Adaptability, from both a personal and professional perspective. Working in the product world can be challenging, so being able to adapt to new technologies or ways of working is a must.

Ultimately, when it comes to UX vs UI, there is no clear winner because this is not a competition. Both specialties are essential parts of the product design process and each has its own unique role to play in creating an enjoyable user experience. It's important for designers to understand both UX design and IxD principles so they can create products that are both usable and beautiful. By understanding how these two areas overlap, you will be able to craft better experiences that truly delight your users! So, to finally put this debate aside – when it comes down to it, UX and UI go hand-in-hand towards creating a great product experience.

From wireframe to prototype

As you learned in the previous chapters, designing a successful product starts with understanding your users and creating an experience that meets their needs. However, once we've successfully concluded our research and completed the discovery process, we need to go into the next phase – the design. The design journey from sketch to coded front-end can often be long and winding, but it doesn't have to be (Figure 7.1).

Once the user research and discovery are complete, it's time to start creating a concept design. Conceptual design is the process of creating basic sketches that outline the structure, layout and content of your website or app. It provides designers with an opportunity to visualize at a high level what the interface will look like and how it might work before committing any resources

FIGURE 7.1   The high-level interaction design process from sketch to code

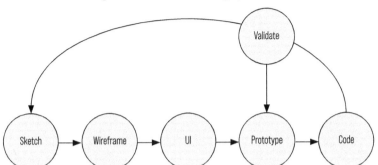

towards UI design, prototyping or coding. Try to view this stage as an exciting transition between conceptual and concrete. This is where you can let your creativity shine. This is the time to use everything you've learned in the discovery phase to start creating the best possible solution.

Personally, I always like to start with sketches on paper just because it enables me to be more creative. The simple act of drawing on paper can do that for you. And don't get me wrong, you don't need to be an artist to do this successfully. In fact, I'm not the best at hand-sketching myself. Many of these sketches will never get in front of anyone (or maybe some will, once you get better at it), but you should use this opportunity to focus on creating the foundations of your future UI. Giorgio Vasari, a 16th-century Italian Renaissance master who worked as a painter, engineer, architect and writer, captures the importance of sketches in a brilliant way:

> These rough sketches, which are born in an instant in the heat of inspiration, express the idea of their author in a few strokes, while on the other hand too much effort and diligence sometimes saps the vitality and powers of those who never know when to leave off.[1]

I personally completely align with this statement. Sketching user interfaces is an art in itself. And I'm not talking about the craft of drawing lines on paper. I'm talking about balancing the time and effort you put into these. As a UX designer, you will have to ask yourself, what are the core informational and visual elements that satisfy your user's needs? How deep in terms of visual detail do you need to go to illustrate your concept? Because this is exactly what you're after here. You're not designing the interface now – you're visualizing the concept.

Sketching is very important in UX because it speeds up your workflow by an order of magnitude (Figure 7.2). This is where many designers get it completely wrong and start this process with a digital tool, then quickly find themselves playing with small, insignificant elements, aligning objects, or even worse going directly into UI design and creating high-fidelity elements before they even know if they're needed. Once you do that, any change that needs to happen (and I want to remind you that change is a constant in design) will take a lot more of your time. It's not worth it at this stage. Sketching on paper also removes an important risk for UX design: distracted stakeholders or users. When discussing or testing early-stage designs, the eye-catching elements of a polished UI design can actually interfere with the user's focus when trying to validate concepts. They might concentrate on the visual elements and give positive feedback when the overall user experience might not be the best. Simply put, they will be distracted by how good-looking the interface is rather than examine how it works and if it fits their needs.

If you're using the sketch to present it to a stakeholder or user for the purpose of gathering information about the overall concept, the sketches on paper are perfectly fine. If, however, you plan to gather feedback about the user journey, basic interactions and layout, I would suggest transferring your sketch to a

FIGURE 7.2   An example of an early sketch for a user interface

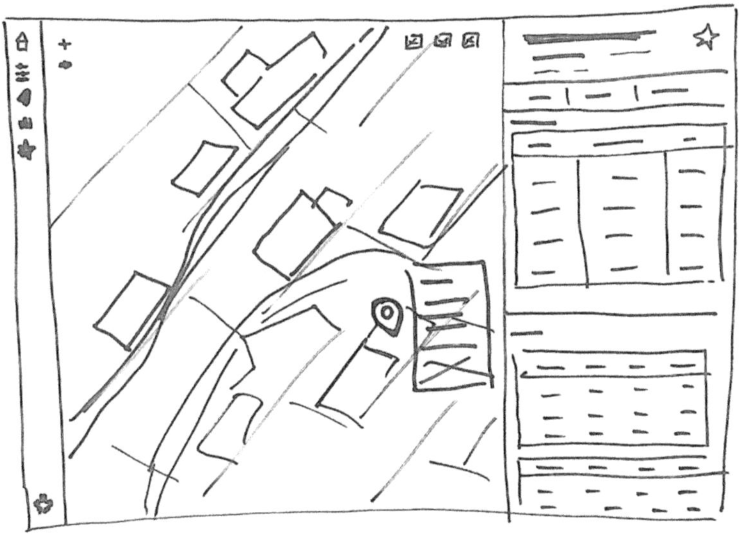

digital medium and testing it on a device your target user is more likely to use. Or, if you want to be even more precise, create a wireframe.

Wireframes

Wireframes are an essential part of the design process. Wireframes are usually created using design tools such as Balsamiq, Figma, Sketch, Adobe XD or Axure. They serve as a visual representation of the product and help to define the structure and layout of the interface. I know what you're going to say: 'But doesn't a sketch do the same thing? Isn't a sketch essentially a wireframe?' I can understand the confusion. In fact, many professional designers will call sketches 'wireframes'. I personally would advise you *not to*, for a simple reason. Sketches and wireframes serve different purposes. While sketches are meant to help the transition from conceptual to concrete and for early design explorations, wireframes can be viewed as early UI designs. Let me explain why. Even at a comparable level of detail (let's assume you have more or less the same elements on the 'screen'), you will already start noticing one thing: they will look and feel different. Why is that? It's because they were essentially created in two different mediums. One physical and one digital. While a sketch on paper is a simulated user interface, a digital wireframe (even if really simple) will already contain user interface properties such as layout, scroll behaviour, basic interactions, etc.

Digital wireframes can help us reveal some early interaction patterns and provide users with a rough idea of how it feels to use the product. The simplest way to think about this is – how are you going to present it to a stakeholder or test it with a user? There's a significant difference between asking them to imagine how the sketch they see on paper will work, and being able to actually interact with it on a screen. However, because UX is a highly creative field, somehow we've managed to create all sorts of quirky variations to sketches and wireframes. A fun example is the notorious 'paper prototype' where crafty designers (literally) take sketches to a whole new level, populating their drawings with data, high-fidelity UI elements and even simulating interactions (I'm always smiling when I see those mobile paper prototypes where you can 'scroll' by dragging a long piece of paper). Ask yourself this: if testing is your goal, why would you not test it in the same medium where the user is actually going to use it – i.e. a computer or mobile screen, where you can also give them access to basic interactions that would feel natural? While these activities can be fun and creative, they pose the risk of attracting the wrong type of feedback.

FIGURE 7.3   An example of a digital wireframe

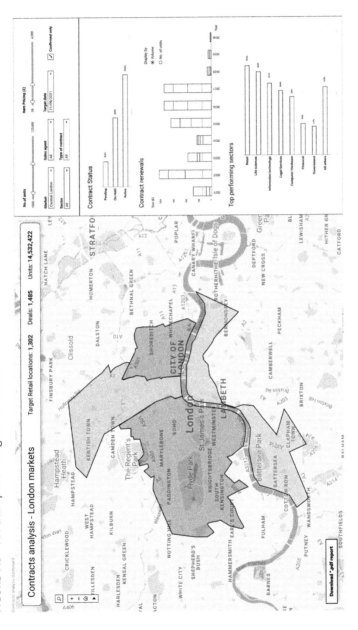

Jake Knapp, designer and author of *Sprint* (which introduced design sprints),[2] seems to agree on this topic in one of his articles titled 'Paper prototyping is a waste of time: Design on paper but always test with a screen'. He goes on to say:

> Has a small child ever showed you artwork made from dried macaroni, glue, and construction paper? No matter what kind of mess you're looking at, you always give the little tyke credit for trying, right?
>
> 'You're so creative! Great effort!'
>
> I've got bad news: If you're using paper prototypes to test a new feature or product, you're probably asking for the same kind of treatment. Starting on paper is great for your design process, but it's a waste of time for research.'[3]

So, a better approach is to test a digital wireframe with a minimal set of UI elements and simple interactions on an actual device. This can help you validate general ideas before investing in UI design or full-blown prototypes. In addition, it's also helpful to catch errors early on while they are still inexpensive to fix. Ultimately, wireframes should be designed with testing in mind.

UI design

You've created your wireframes and flows, and validated them with target users, so the time has come to actually design and build high-fidelity UI screens or mock-ups. Depending on how your product is set up, this can take more or less time. I could write an entire book on how design systems can speed up this step, but that is not my goal here. Just keep in mind that, depending on the resources you have at hand, this process can look slightly different. Design system or not, you will have to start with a UI design tool like Figma and carefully build up all the necessary screens that power your product. This involves creating the visual elements of the product, including layouts, colour schemes, typography, icons and images. The visual design is the step where the product starts to come to life, and as a UX designer you will create high-fidelity mock-ups of the product's interface. You will have to focus on creating a visually appealing and consistent design that aligns with the brand's guidelines, with business goals and meets the target audience's needs.

As I mentioned before in this section, this step doesn't just cover visual elements of the user interface but also covers important elements like content (copy, micro-copy, videos, etc.), sound, voice and so on. This is where you are trying to get to a level of fidelity that will be close to the final product. We do this so we can accurately test how users respond to the newly created experience. I dedicate more space to this topic in the next couple of sections where I talk about the fidelity levels of your design and go into more detail about how to create good user interfaces.

As a final step, you should also review these designs with your stakeholders from the business, product and engineering teams, presenting them with the user's feedback and proposing the final design. This is perhaps the last stage where you can do this in an inexpensive way. Anything that comes after will involve a lot more work to re-factor (particularly when you reach the coding phase), so view this as an important opportunity to make any last-minute improvements.

Prototyping

Remember when I said UX design isn't a linear process? Well, this is a very good example of that. Even though, for simplicity, I'm presenting it here in a linear way, it doesn't mean you will follow these steps in a linear way in a real product environment. Let me give you an example. Let's say you've sketched your concept and then proceeded to build wireframes for a mobile application you're working on. You are happy with the flow, and everything looks solid, but you are unsure how users will react to a couple of features you are proposing that you've developed from initial user research. Does it mean you need to build up the entire high-fidelity UI and prototype it before you test that assumption? No way! Always look at this process as a balance between time spent and potential ROI or risks. Is it worth waiting for high-fidelity mock-ups? In most cases, I would say no. Wireframes, if done at the right fidelity level, can do the job. I'll go into more detail about what the right fidelity means in the next section, but what you need to understand now is one thing: deciding when and at what fidelity level you need to prototype depends on the hypothesis you want to test. For that, you first need a hypothesis. This and the complexity of your product will dictate whether you can test with simple wireframes with limited content and interactions or whether you need to design more realistic mock-ups and even include advanced interactivity. It's a balance.

Another important reason why prototypes are crucial for UX design is the fact that you get a chance to test the entire user experience, rather than just individual screens. Essentially, your users can get to experience how everything fits together. Prototypes are basically an early version of the final product, which helps everyone involved better visualize and evaluate the design. Prototypes can also provide developers with more accurate information on how elements interact and link together so they can start thinking about and even developing some of the building blocks. And this is what usually happens in real-life situations. The development team isn't going to wait until you've completed all designs and validated everything, and only then start work. That would be the wrong approach anyway. Instead, what successful teams are doing is evaluating the user experience and identifying those elements that are highly unlikely to change. Usually, this means starting with infrastructure elements such as databases, integration with third parties and automation, but it's not limited to that. By having prototypes, you are enabling the entire product development team to work in parallel, essentially speeding up the entire process.

Coding

Finally, this last step might seem like an obvious one, but there is some advice I would like to share with you. Once you feel comfortable with the designs, and we've made sure we have validated them with both the users and the business, it's time to hand them over to the product and development team. Sounds pretty straightforward, right? In reality, this is where things can get tricky.

On many occasions, I've seen development teams getting utterly confused at this stage. This usually happens for a few reasons, and I would like to highlight some of those to you to you so you can try to avoid making these mistakes:

- *You haven't taken your team on the journey.* Stakeholders from the development team were not part of the discovery process. This means very important technical limitations might have been missed, and you've designed a solution that is not feasible. This can end up being very costly for the business as well.
- *This is the first time they have seen your designs.* While it can be tempting to hide away in a room and create like an artist until you feel ready to show your masterpiece to the world, it also means no one else has had the chance to give you any feedback on it, and you could be missing out on amazing ideas.
- *You haven't documented and properly handed over your designs.* I can't stress this enough. Your job doesn't end with the last component added on a Figma screen. Please remember to document your design, fleshing out interactions and flows, component behaviours, technical expectations, etc. Don't expect the development team to just 'get it'. While you have been working on this for quite some time, they haven't and will be less familiar with how everything works and fits together. Your product and development team will thank you for this.
- *You haven't created a shared space that makes handing over easier* and can act as a single source of truth for the product.

Figma, for example, makes this very easy. Developers can have access to a shared board and can ask questions directly on your proposed designs. This has a different use than Jira, where you will discuss more granular, sprint related issues. Also, don't share all your design files with the development team. Even if it's good for them to see all your design explorations or in-progress work, this might sometimes cause confusion.

Following the sketch to wireframe to prototype approach is essential for your businesses and users alike. By creating a wireframe, you can quickly and inexpensively test different design options and identify any potential problems with the layout or structure or the overall value proposition of the product. Creating a prototype is also equally important. By allowing users to interact with the interface as if it were a finished product, you can gather feedback on the functionality and usability of the interface.

It's important to follow this process as it allows you, your developers, product manager and business stakeholders to catch any usability issues early on and make corrections before investing time in designing visuals or coding an interface. By taking these steps, you will save a great deal of time and resources in the long run, as changes can be made quickly and easily before one single line of code needs to be written. All in all, sketching, wireframing and prototyping are key for successful products.

Fidelity

Now it's the appropriate time to dive into this very important topic. When it comes to UX design, 'fidelity' refers to how closely a user interface will look and behave compared to the final product that we're about to deliver. This can range from simple wireframes to realistic visual and interactive mock-ups, and everything in between. Largely, there are two types of fidelity: low-fidelity design, which may be a wireframe or sketch; and high-fidelity design, which may resemble the real-life product and its behaviour.[4]

I'm mentioning behaviour because when I talk about fidelity, I'm not just referring to the visuals. There are many more elements that can go into increasing the fidelity of a design. Two good examples are:

- *Interaction patterns.* What happens when users engage with certain element in the product? Are there micro interactions included, like animations, sounds or other interface feedback?
- *Content.* The 'fidelity' of the content needed will depend on the type of product. Say, for example, you want to test an interface for financial advisers. As you can imagine, *Lorem ipsum* is not going to do the job.

But why does selecting the appropriate fidelity matter? When designing, the goal is always to deliver an experience that users value. Achieving this requires careful consideration of the user needs, business and product goals, timeline, resources and budget – all of which should inform your decision on what level of fidelity is most suitable within each stage of the UX process. You are essentially trying to be frugal in terms of resources.

And how do we select the appropriate fidelity when we have to consider so many elements? Choosing the right level of fidelity for a user interface really comes down to the stage of the design process and the specific needs of the product in that stage. What do I mean by this? You will have to ask yourself one question at all times: 'What am I trying to achieve in this phase?' What is your goal? Is it to explore a concept? Is it to test a user interface with users? Is it to hand over designs to the development team? As I mentioned before, it also depends a lot on the type of product you are designing and the context. There is a huge difference between designing a restaurant app and an enterprise banking application. The level of fidelity and the

FIGURE 7.4 Different fidelity levels in UX design

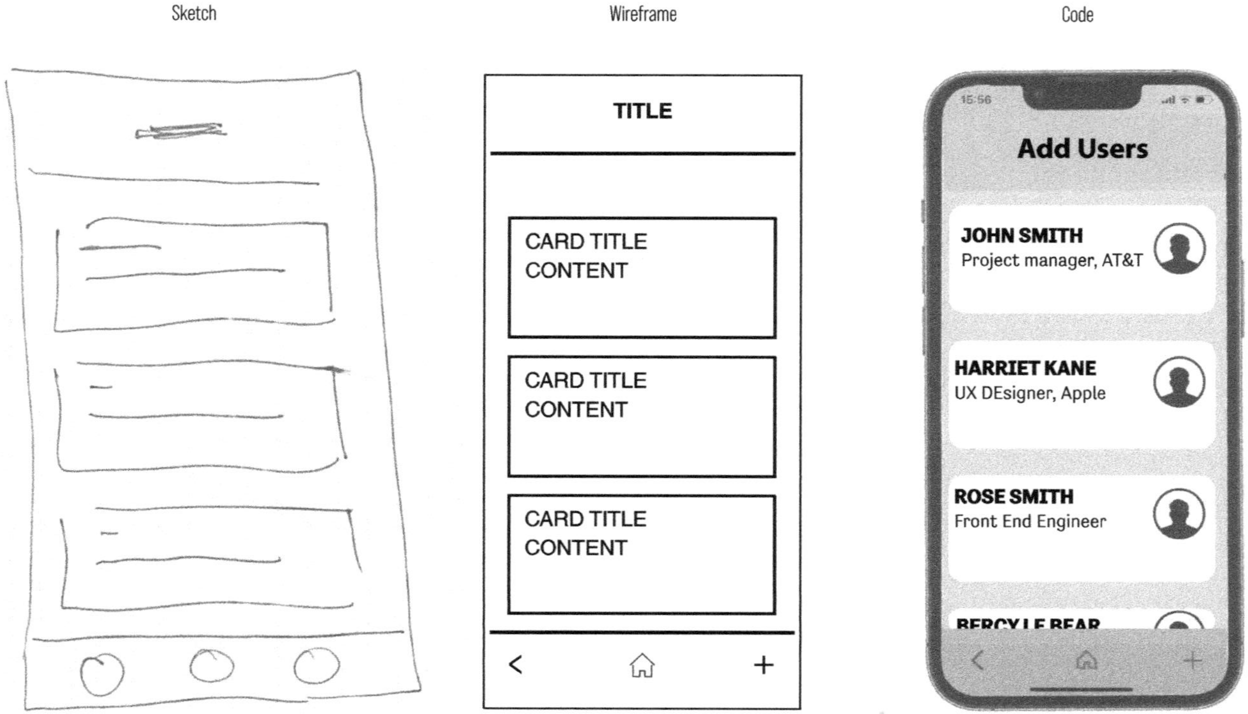

Sketch

Wireframe

Code

TITLE

CARD TITLE
CONTENT

CARD TITLE
CONTENT

CARD TITLE
CONTENT

Add Users

16:56

JOHN SMITH
Project manager, AT&T

HARRIET KANE
UX DEsigner, Apple

ROSE SMITH
Front End Engineer

PERCY LE REAR

realism of content needed to test your designs are vastly different, so to evaluate them successfully you will need to make adjustments based on that.

As you might have noticed, I left testing out of the list of things we need to think about when choosing the fidelity level we need. I did this on purpose, because testing needs to have its own special place. It's probably the single most important reason why we even have fidelity levels, otherwise, if not for user testing, everything would always be high-fidelity and ready to be handed over to the development team. The reason why I left it out was because I wanted to stress one important thing: it's not enough to just say you're going to test your design with users and then change the fidelity level based on that – you need to make sure that you are testing a hypothesis, not 'everything'. Testing everything, means there no focus and no way to know what fidelity level you actually need. The hypothesis in simple terms is essentially *what* you want to test. I will cover this topic in more detail later in Chapter 8, but, to give an example, you might need to test a product that is meant for stockbrokers. Let's assume you've defined your main hypothesis as 'Users want to be able to compare multiple stocks values on the same chart by colour'. Now, if we look at that hypothesis statement alone, we can learn two things: we'll need to use realistic data, and our fidelity level needs to include colours. This is a very good example of a situation where low fidelity would simply not work because our hypothesis dictates that. We will need high-fidelity content (numbers) and visual representations of stocks that actually make sense. I always advise using real or close-to-real data in any of your designs. We are also likely to need a high-fidelity user interface. The charts will probably need to be very precise, and interactions should be present so the user can select the desired stocks, so the comparison feels dynamic. All these aspects point to our need to build high-fidelity screens and prototypes.

Now that you've hopefully understood how this works, I'll conclude this section with one thing I'm always telling designers in my team, and that I would like you to remember: in reality, there's no high or low-fidelity, just *appropriate fidelity*.

Designing user interfaces

In this section, I will focus on the user interface (UI) design phase of IxD. As you might expect, I'm going to talk less about specific buttons or hamburger menus and more about the core principles of UI design.

Designing user interfaces is a creative and demanding process that requires you to know your tools, understand how the UI will work with the user and develop a design that powers the user experience you have in mind. This is not to say that you don't have to know your tools when doing research or concept exploration, but more that this particular phase is much more reliant on digital tools. While you can probably design a fantastic user experience just using pen and paper, I can't say the same for a high-fidelity user interface. You must get familiar with the tools. This is because, unlike everything else UX, UI does have an artistic component to it. In theory, a user experience, once designed, is a constant, a framework, but the user interface that powers that experience can look vastly different depending on who designs it. This shell can look different depending on the designer. In fact, you can sometimes achieve more or less the same user experience by using very different user interfaces. This phase of UX gets a bit blurry because although there are clear principles and processes we follow, designing visual interfaces will always include an element of personal touch and subjectivity.

So, does that mean designing a UI is an art? Yes and no. Yes, because designers can craft the user interface in new and innovative ways and are able to use their creativity and artistic flair. And no, because designing user interfaces involves more than just aesthetic appeal. It requires consideration of user research, business goals, data, context, etc. When designers don't pay attention to these details, the result can often be an interface that is visually appealing but fails to deliver the intended user experience.

So, UI design can be complex, but there are some principles that are essential for creating effective user interfaces. Here are, in my opinion, three of the most important ones for UI design.

Functionality

This is perhaps the most important principle of UI design and the element that distinguishes UI design the most from other disciplines like illustration or graphic design. The interface should *always* be designed with the user's needs and goals in mind, and it should be straightforward for them to navigate and complete tasks. The UI should also be designed with the product as a whole in mind, including any constraints or limitations that may impact the user's experience.

Usability

Usability refers to how easy it is for your user to utilize the interface. The interface you design should be intuitive and easy to learn, with clear visual cues and a logical layout. You'll need to consider the user's cognitive load by not presenting them with too much information at the same time, and aim to reduce the mental effort required to complete tasks. Finally, you should also consider the user's environment, such as the device and context in which they will be using the product (e.g. it is likely that a physical exercise tracking app will be used outside, on the move and on a mobile device).

Aesthetics

Last but not least, aesthetics refers to the overall feel of the interface's visual design. The UI should be visually pleasing, with a consistent style and an appropriate colour scheme that matches the branding. Great UI design requires an understanding of typography, colour, space and hierarchy – all of which need to be balanced and coherent. As a designer, you will also need to consider the user's emotional response to the interface and aim to create a positive experience. You will also need to take into account the product as a whole and aim to maintain consistency with other marketing materials and brand assets.

By following these three core principles, you can create a cohesive and effective user interface that meets the user's needs and enhances their overall experience. But what happens when you don't do that? 'Luckily', other designers made these mistakes before, so you don't have to. Here is a list of the top blunders to avoid when designing a user interface:

- *Not considering user experience.* Designing a nice-looking interface without taking into account the user experience you've spent so long researching and planning is a sure way to create a bad UI. I started with this because it's probably the worst offence and one of the most encountered problems, unfortunately.

- *Over-designing the UI.* This is when you're creating an overly complicated or cluttered interface. This can happen when the designer tries to include too many decorative visual elements or features in the product, making it difficult for users to navigate and find what they need. Keep in mind that simple and clean is always better.

- *Creating content overload.* Reading long chunks of text, examining endless rows of data or looking at tens of photos and videos on one screen can be tedious and tiring for the user, so it's essential to keep the amount of information on one screen minimal and only include what's absolutely necessary. Otherwise, you run the risk of creating cognitive overload. This can be avoided by using techniques such as progressive disclosure or information layering.

- *No visual hierarchy.* Designing an eye-catching UI without a consistent visual hierarchy will make the interface confusing and hard to navigate. Visual hierarchy helps users understand which elements are the most important on a screen and how to navigate them. Visual hierarchy is one of the most important and overlooked aspects of UI design. If done well, it's invisible to the user but creates an amazing user experience.
- *Poor responsiveness.* Imagine you're working on a web app with half of your users likely to use mobile devices to access it, and it's not working. Responsive design is essential for ensuring your application looks good and works well across different devices and screen sizes.
- *No or inadequate testing.* I hope I don't even need to tell you how bad an idea not testing your designs is, so I'll skip to the next one: inadequate testing. This is another UI design blunder. This can happen when the UX designer does not test the product with the right group of users or does not test with a diverse enough group. Without adequate testing, issues with the interface may go unnoticed until after the product is released.

Just to wrap up, designing good user interfaces is a critical aspect of creating successful digital products. The UX design process involves creating a visual design, user interactions and refining the interface based on feedback from user testing sessions. I advise you to try to follow the best practices and, together with using the right tools, you can create the most engaging and intuitive user interfaces that stand the test of time.

Accessibility and inclusive design

Accessibility is not a buzzword, it's a vitally important aspect of UX design that often gets overlooked. The reason for that is in most cases the budget. While everyone recognizes the value of accessibility, not many organizations are actually prepared to invest in it, thinking that this would save costs. Designing accessible products is not easy, but that doesn't necessarily mean it needs to be prohibitively expensive. In fact, in this section I will show you how following a few best practices can cover a lot of the ground work needed for an accessible product.

Whether you're designing for a global enterprise or a small start-up, it's important to consider users with different needs and abilities – and start promoting and implementing accessible design. If you're not already thinking about accessibility, you're missing out on a potential audience and creating barriers for people with disabilities.

To start, let's consider what we mean by accessibility. Accessibility can be described as the creation of items, products, systems or places that are accessible to all people, particularly those with disabilities. The goal of accessibility is to make sure that individuals who experience disabilities have an equal opportunity to access information and services available in their environment. I would like to note that these considerations benefit not only disabled persons but in fact everyone involved!

So, how can you design accessible user interfaces without a major investment? Here are my top tips that don't require a massive effort to implement:

- *Provide users with alternative text for images.* For people who use screen readers or who cannot see the images, alternative text (sometimes referred to as alt tags or alt text) provides a description of the image that can be read aloud or displayed on the screen.
- *Design with colour contrast in mind.* This is important for people with visual impairments to be able to read your content. There are various online tools that can help you ensure that the colour contrast in your product meets the recommended accessibility standards.

- *Use descriptive link text.* Instead of using generic link text like 'Click here', using descriptive text that explains where the link goes can help people who use screen readers or who have cognitive disabilities understand the purpose of the link. For example, in this case using 'Click here to access your account information' as your descriptive text can really make a difference.
- *Create clear and simple content.* Might seem like an obvious one, but you would be surprised how little consideration many product teams give to this aspect. So, try to avoid using technical jargon and complicated words that may be difficult to understand for people with cognitive disabilities. And, of course, all your users will benefit from this.
- *Create good hierarchy for your content.* Proper headings and formatting make it easier for people who use screen readers or who have cognitive disabilities to understand the structure and hierarchy of your content.
- *Design products with keyboard accessibility.* This is the practice of ensuring that users with physical or cognitive impairments can still access and interact with your product by using only a keyboard. This means making sure all interactive elements, such as buttons, links and forms are accessible via keyboard shortcuts.

By following these tips, you can make sure your product is more accessible without needing huge teams or budgets. And the best part? These tips will make your product better for everyone, not just people with disabilities.

But accessibility is just one side of the coin. Another equally important topic I want to discuss is inclusive design, which is a set of 'methodologies to create products that understand and enable people of all backgrounds and abilities. It may address accessibility, age, economic situation, geographic location, language, race, and more.'[5] Inclusive design goes beyond simply removing barriers to accessibility, and instead aims to create products that are welcoming and easy to use for all users. Design inclusivity can be achieved in many ways, such as using inclusive language and imagery, considering the diversity of your user base when designing your product, and avoiding stereotypes and biases in your design. By creating products that are inclusive, you can create a better user experience for everyone.

While accessibility and design inclusivity are distinct concepts, they both play an essential role in ensuring that your product is accessible to a broad range of users – including those with disabilities. By designing for accessibility, you can ensure that everyone's abilities are taken into account when designing the product. At the same time, by designing for inclusion, it becomes more inviting and straightforward to use, regardless of one's background or capabilities.

Notes

1   Google Arts and Culture. Giorgio Vasari, Jul 30, 1511–Jun 27, 1574, Google Arts and Culture, nd. artsandculture.google.com/entity/giorgio-vasari/m0pvnq (archived at https://perma.cc/ND84-62FB)

2   J Knapp (2016) *Sprint: How to solve big problems and test new ideas in just five days*, Simon & Schuster, New York

3   J Knapp. Paper prototyping is a waste of time: Design on paper but always test with a screen, GV Library, 26 March 2014. library.gv.com/paper-prototyping-is-a-waste-of-time-353076395187#.2svlh4vf5 (archived at https://perma.cc/3U68-7KMH)

4   K Pernice. UX prototypes: Low fidelity vs high fidelity, NN/g, 18 December 2016. www.nngroup.com/articles/ux-prototype-hi-lo-fidelity (archived at https://perma.cc/KR54-ZLVU)

5   A Joyce. Inclusive design, NN/g, 30 January 2022. www.nngroup.com/articles/inclusive-design (archived at https://perma.cc/UNV7-XWVK)

CHAPTER EIGHT

Evaluating UX

You've designed and prototyped your solution. The user interface looks and feels fantastic, and the team is impressed and eager to start coding it. But before you move forward, it is important to find out whether it actually resonates with your target users. If you remember from the previous chapter, having an eye-catching UI is rarely enough. You need to make sure your designs work in the real world. Evaluating the user experience helps assess a product's usability and quality by collecting feedback from actual users. This can help you identify any areas that need improvement or where users may be confused. You can also verify whether the team has hit its desired goals for the product.

I've dedicated this chapter to exploring various methods for evaluating user experiences, such as heuristic evaluation, usability testing, surveying, etc., and their respective benefits and limitations. Additionally, we'll examine the role of metrics and analytics in evaluating user experience and how they can be used to measure success or failure. We'll discuss why evaluating the user experience is essential for successful products, and I'll share examples of how these techniques can be applied effectively in your day-to-day work. By the end of this chapter, I trust you will have a better understanding of how to evaluate user experience in order to start coding them confidently.

Heuristics evaluation

Heuristic evaluation is a popular technique used in the field of UX design to assess the usability of a product or service. The term 'heuristics' 'comes from the Greek word *heurisko*, which means 'to discover' or to 'find out'. In computer science and cognitive psychology, a heuristic is a problem-solving strategy that uses practical methods to find solutions to complex problems. Heuristics were first introduced in the field of psychology in the 1970s, and they have since been used in a variety of fields, including engineering, business and design.

The meaning and use that we're most interested in were first introduced by Jakob Nielsen and Rolf Molich in 1990 as an alternative to traditional usability testing methods, which were time-consuming and expensive. Heuristic evaluation is based on a set of guidelines, known as heuristics, that are used to evaluate a product's usability. Whenever you hear the term heuristics with regard to usability and UX, it's highly likely that it will be in one way or another tied to Nielsen's 10 usability heuristics, which were first introduced in 1994. These heuristics are widely used today and are considered by many to be the industry standard for evaluating the usability of a product or service.[1]

But let's dive in and see what each of these heuristics means, and provide some real-world examples so they're easier to understand. For consistency, I'm going to name the exact titles of each heuristic as Jakob Nielsen used them.

1 *Visibility of system status.* This refers to the fact that the user must be always kept up to speed in terms of what is happening

with the system they are using. Whenever a user interacts with the interface, feedback should be given by the system through appropriate means within a reasonable time. For example, if the user clicks a button to complete an action, the system should give feedback and inform the user wherever or not that action was successful. This is one of the most important heuristics that you need to watch out for. Imagine what would happen if, for example, you are shortlisting an item for your online shopping, but the system doesn't give you any feedback. As a user, you will wonder: 'Did that actually work?', 'Did it go through?', 'Maybe I didn't click the button', 'Maybe I should try again', etc. As you can imagine, this can cause great confusion for the user. Always be on the watch for this heuristic because it's a foundational one.

2 *Match between system and the real world.* This heuristic talks about the fact that the product should be designed to communicate with the user in a way that is familiar to them and that they understand. It is essential to utilize words, behaviours and concepts that are recognizable to them instead of terms exclusive to the product's operations. The best example I can think of is the Uber app. As a user, you are presented with high-level, friendly information, essentially all you need to know in order to get from point A to point B without the headaches. Imagine what would happen if the system started exposing to you how the transactions are being settled in the background, with which banks, how the drivers are getting incentivized or how the system calculates the fastest route. You don't need or want that.

3 *User control and freedom.* Imagine being in your favourite work app, updating some important information, and by mistake you delete all your work. How would you feel if the system told you to contact support on the phone, and they'll help you out with reinstating your data? Sounds like a bit of a nightmare coming your way, doesn't it? This heuristic talks about the fact that user actions need to be easily and quickly

reversible, otherwise they produce instant frustrations for the user.

4 *Consistency and standards.* This heuristic describes how users should not have to wonder whether different interaction patterns, words, behaviours or imagery mean the same thing as they do somewhere else. Following well-established conventions is the safest way. This is also backed up by Jakob's Law, which states that 'users spend most of their time on other websites than your website'.[2]

5 *Error prevention.* This is a golden one. As a UX designer, it's important to present your user with interface feedback (e.g. errors, warnings), but it's even more important to try to prevent those issues from occurring in the first place. Myself, I love data, so I'm going to give you an example of how this heuristic, if followed, can improve data quality. Let's say somewhere in your product you have an input field for a date. Now, you could use this date field in a certain format (let's assume MM/DD/YYYY), but then you would have to design error messages in case the user enters it wrong, the development team will have to include validations, and users who use a different date format (DD/MM/YYYY) will get confused. Or, by applying this heuristic in advance, you could use a calendar picker component. No more errors, no more warnings. You've just made sure that you are validating the data at source. This just proves how choosing the right interaction pattern can be instrumental to a good UX.

6 *Recognition rather than recall.* This heuristic is about design consistency. Think about the visual components you will use, the layout, the typography, colours, etc., and make sure they are consistent throughout your product. Reduce the user's cognitive load by displaying objects, actions and options in a clear manner. Instructions for the product should be visible or easily retrievable whenever needed by the user.

7 *Flexibility and efficiency of use.* Accelerators – unseen to the eye of a novice user – may often speed up the interaction for the expert user. These are basically shortcuts in the user experience that are sometimes unintended. They are usually encountered in complex and non-linear user experiences where it's almost impossible to anticipate every potential path a user will take. Design the user experience in a way that can cater to both inexperienced and experienced users. Allow users to tailor frequently used features to their needs.

8 *Aesthetic and minimalist design.* It is essential that interfaces do not contain unnecessary or infrequently used data, to ensure an efficient user experience. Any additional information can create unwanted information overload. You can avoid this by adopting a minimalist design with a solid information hierarchy, and the overall user experience will be a pleasant one.

9 *Help users recognize, diagnose and recover from errors.* 'Warning! Error 14104', 'Ok/Cancel'. Now, that doesn't sound really helpful, does it? This heuristic focuses on providing our users with friendly error messages that allow them to understand what went wrong and be able to fix it quickly. Key here will be the language and content you use in your error patterns. So instead of 'Error 14104' maybe use a more natural language, for example, 'Poor network connectivity detected. Your file failed to upload'. 'Cancel/Retry'. Now that's much better, no?

10 *Help and documentation.* In an ideal world, the user experience you've designed would not need any explanation. But sometimes, due to the complexity of the product, it may be necessary to provide help and documentation. Any such information should be accessible to search, focused on the user's needs, list steps to be carried out and not be too lengthy.

Ok, we've tried to make sense of each of these heuristics, but how do you actually use them to evaluate UX? The process is quite simple. In order for this to work effectively, you will need to select a group of evaluators that will examine the user experience of your product through the lens of the heuristics we've presented. Why do we need more than one person? 'Surely I could just do it myself', you might say. Statistically speaking, it's close to impossible for a single individual to find every usability issue in the product, even following Nielsen's heuristics. The output from this method is a list of usability issues found by the evaluators.

I've started with heuristics as the main method for evaluating UX, not because it's the most used but because it's the most inexpensive one. If your evaluators are also domain experts, there's a higher chance they will catch any potential usability issues that are impacting your product. Another big advantage of this method is that it provides a consistent and repeatable way of evaluating the usability of a product or service. Of course, there are other types of heuristics available in the design field, such as cognitive walkthroughs, Arhippainen's ten user experience heuristics, Shneiderman's eight golden rules of interface design and many more. Feel free to explore these as well because it will give you a lot more insight into why heuristics are vital for evaluating user experience.

Usability testing

When it comes to evaluating user experience, usability testing or user testing is often the most reliable method. I would go even further than that and say it's also a non-negotiable one, or, in other words, 'we aren't doing user experience design if we haven't actually seen a user experience it.'[3] This technique involves exposing a user to a product or service and observing their interactions with it. User testing can take many forms, each of which offers some unique advantages and disadvantages. In this section, I'll go into a bit more detail on each of these. We'll also learn what are the steps to complete a successful user testing session.

Usability tests are usually performed under controlled conditions by recruiting participants whose characteristics match the target user group of the product. The results from the user tests can be used to identify potential usability issues related to user interface design, content organization, navigation flow, etc., which can be used to make user experience improvements.

There are multiple types of user testing, depending on our goals, the context and the way we administer the test. In Chapter 5 we've been discussing some of the basics. Now it's time to go into a bit more detail and try to understand the differences between them.

Remote testing

This is the most cost-efficient and time-saving way to conduct usability tests, allowing testers from any location to take part in the process. These tests are administered online by making sure they have a predefined structure and clear steps for the user to follow. These are usually in the form of tasks the user has to complete using a prototype of your product or even the live product itself. Because the tasks have a goal and a path to follow, we can quantify the success rate of each of those tasks to give us an indication of what works and what doesn't. You can also measure the time it took each participant to complete a task, thus evaluating how 'agile' your user experience is. Depending on how big the sample size is, the confidence levels in the results can increase or decrease.

Advantages:

- Participants can test the product in their natural environment, making this test closer to a real-life situation and, as a result, increasing your confidence in the findings.

- It's easier to recruit participants since some people prefer not to travel or feel more comfortable doing this from their preferred location.
- It's easier to find suitable timeslots with your participants when the tests are being administered online.
- It saves time and cost for everyone involved.

Disadvantages:

- Since the test is going to be online, there will be limited interaction between the facilitator and the participants. This can sometimes mean that you will miss behavioural cues, gestures or other small details that could actually end up being very important.
- As with any online test, participants might face technical difficulties that can prevent them from completing the tasks.

When to use:

- Use remote testing when you have a limited usability testing budget. This will allow you to still gather lots of valuable information on how users will interact with your product. It's also important to note that remote testing can be scaled to more participants in a shorter period of time, thus enabling you to gather more data.

In-person testing

By having participants come in person to do the usability testing, you will be able to gain a deeper understanding of their behaviour and receive more insightful feedback. This kind of testing will be, by nature, slightly more challenging to plan and administer, and you are likely to need a more substantial budget.

Advantages:

- Being able to observe non-visual cues, behaviours, gestures, etc., that would otherwise be 'invisible' in a remote test environment.
- You have the chance to ask your participants more focused questions compared to online tests.

Disadvantages:

- More costly and time-consuming for the product team to set up and manage.
- Challenges with setting up location. Participants need to be given directions, potential delays, transport costs, etc.
- Harder to scale, as it's almost impossible to have back-to-back sessions.

When to use:

- Use in-person testing when you plan to go deeper into a certain area of usability. For example, when you want to test a newly launched feature and want to learn as much as possible about that without necessarily looking at the entire product for usability issues. By having the chance to ask live questions and adapt the interview based on the direction it goes you have a higher chance of discovering issues or opportunities that otherwise would be hard with remote testing.

High-level remote testing

At a high level, remote testing can be done in two different ways: moderated or unmoderated. Let's have a closer look at how these two compare.

- *Remote moderated testing* is very similar to in-person testing. This kind of research technique provides UX designers with an opportunity to acquire further, more sophisticated feedback from remote participants. The session is usually led by a moderator or facilitator who will allow for questions to be answered along the way. The obvious difference between a remote testing session and an in-person one is the medium where the interaction takes place. While this can be more convenient to arrange, as no travel or setting up of a physical test environment is required, it will present the moderator with reduced ways to interact with the participant, particularly in terms of non-verbal cues. Simply put, it's a lot more difficult to communicate and 'even a clever observer of human emotions will be faced with a great deal of noise or communicational interference. We can all expect to look a lot clumsier, more awkward, and anxious than we would in the physical world.'[4]

- *Remote unmoderated testing*. While remote moderated tests are a bit of an in-between state, this type of testing, on the other hand, has two very clear purposes: to reduce costs and to enable more quantitative usability data to be gathered. This is where you care more about how well participants can perform the tasks you assign to them in terms of time to complete and success rate. That is not to say you can't still gather qualitative data, as you can encourage people to voice their thoughts as they go through the exercises, but it will feel less natural to them, and some will tend not to share their real opinions. So while you will be gaining in terms of budget and scalability, being able to run larger studies at a reduced cost, you will be losing the ability to ask more questions at key moments in time. This type of test also opens up new avenues for automation by using online tools such as Maze.co, UserZoom.com, UserTesting.com and many others that will also provide you with a quantitative data report at the end of the study, saving precious time and collating all insights.

Principles of usability studies

Next, I would like to share with you some simple principles that will allow you to make sure you are conducting a successful usability study no matter the type of method you choose:

- *Always define goals for your study.* This might seem like a no-brainer, but you'd be amazed at how many UX designers don't give this one the necessary attention. By not setting goals for your study you run the risk of going in too broad and losing track of what you want to achieve. With no focus, your interviews are going to touch on every aspect of your product, and may not even be relevant to you at that time. So, always start by defining the goals of the test. The goals should be *specific, measurable, and realistic.* I can't stress enough how important these three aspects are. It will allow you to focus on key areas, measure outcomes in a structured way and benchmark results.

- *Plan your study.* Once you have defined your goals, it's time to create a plan that outlines the testing method, tasks and questions. Start with choosing the type of test that is most likely to allow you to reach your goals, plan your tasks out accordingly and make sure you write clear and concise questions and directions. It doesn't matter whether the test will be in person or remote, it always helps to have written materials to make sure every test follows the same structure. This will enable you to better measure outcomes after.

- *Recruit participants.* Yet another obvious one, you might say. Ok, fair enough. Just make sure you are doing it properly. Only recruit participants that match your target user group. Testing with people outside that group will most likely result in false positive results that, down the line, can lead to disastrous consequences for your product. Also, make sure that, even within your target group, you are recruiting a diverse set of people with different backgrounds, genders and other relevant characteristics.

- *Run the test.* When running the test, I suggest that you make sure you don't introduce bias in the conversation and make sure you don't lead your participants into giving certain answers. Conduct the test according to the test plan you set up earlier and try not to deviate from it. Always record the participants' behaviour and feedback so you can go back later and watch/listen to the test again. From my experience, re-watching the session can reveal many insights you haven't captured the first time. Also, having someone to capture insights while you run the interview can give much better results. Never take notes during the interview. Focus on the user and what they are doing. You will have enough time later.

- *Analyse the results.* Analysing data from usability tests can be a tedious task if, for example, you haven't created a clear structure for your interview. This will also make analysing data from multiple sessions very hard. My advice is never to run 'freestyle' sessions hoping for the best. Having a script, clear questions and a structured approach will mean it will be easier to collect and analyse the data from the test and draw conclusions based on the findings.

- *Prioritize and implement changes.* Once you've concluded your analysis, you will have a list of findings. Now, don't go jumping into implementing all of those! This is the time to spend some time with your product team and prioritize all findings based on impact on the business, technical complexity and potential ROI. Create and design solutions for those findings and, finally, implement them to make improvements to the product.

Usability testing is an invaluable component of the design process, as it enables designers to acquire insight from real users. This feedback allows them to make strategic adjustments in order to craft a product that satisfies user expectations and requirements. Usability testing can identify UX issues, provide ways for improvement and create products with superior usability features, ultimately resulting in improved quality and enhanced user experiences. For any designer who plans on creating excellent digital products, incorporating usability tests into their workflow is paramount!

Evaluating UX through product analytics

The time has come to launch your product to the big wide world. What an exciting moment! But in order to keep this fantastic journey progressing, you need to consistently monitor the user experience. Product analytics offer an ideal way of tracking how users interact with your product and do this on multiple dimensions. Not only that, but with the available technology today, you can basically see live how your people are using your product. This is incredibly important because you can convert these detailed insights into necessary improvements or even breakthroughs that can present immense value down the road. As long as user experience remains a top priority for your product, incremental growth is not just possible but a must in today's product world.

But what exactly are product analytics? Atlassian, the parent company of Jira and Confluence, two industry-standard tools, defines it as 'the process of analyzing how users engage with a product or service. It enables product teams to *track, visualize, and analyze* user engagement and behavior data. Teams use this data to improve and optimize a product or service.'[5] I really prefer this definition over all the other ones I've encountered for one simple reason: it goes right at the core of what product analytics means: tracking user behaviour, visualizing the data and analysing the data to extract insights.

All product teams need to understand and use analytics in order to make informed decisions about their products. In today's highly competitive environment, this is a must. This data can be used to improve usability, the user experience and the overall chances of success for a product. There are many different types of product analytics that are available to use. As a UX designer, it's important to be able to use these analytics to understand how users interact with your product. However, it can be difficult to know where to start, so let me shed some light on this topic. In this section, I will go through the types of analytics most commonly used for evaluating user experience and how to utilize them effectively.

Product metrics

Before we take a closer look at product analytics, you first need to understand what product metrics are. Product metrics are actionable indicators used to track a product's performance and progress towards desired objectives. 'Objectives' is the keyword here – to successfully track a product's progress, you first need to define the metrics you want to measure. Conversion rates, customer acquisition cost, monthly recurring revenue, etc., are just some of the potential measurements that illustrate this concept. Metrics rely on data collected through analytics tools for accuracy, and this is where these two concepts (product metrics and product analytics) become closely tied together in practice. One feeds the other.

So, while product metrics and product analytics have similarities, they are not one and the same. But let's be more precise: product analytics refers to obtaining data regarding a service or product for further examination; this process is usually done by using various methods such as user tracking, trends analysis, cohort analysis, journey analysis, etc. Once gathered, this data can enable us to gain knowledge about how our users engage with the products we offer, as well as what kind of outcomes it could bring forth for our business. By using insights collected through product analytics, we can make better decisions on how to continue developing our products while also enhancing the overall user experience.

Product metrics can be organized into five main categories: acquisition, activation, engagement, retention and monetization.[6] But what do they mean?

- *Acquisition.* This measures the number of new people using your product or service. User acquisition metrics are essential because they help the product team to understand which channels are working best, and which cohorts of users are performing better and can inform your future user acquisition strategy.

- *Activation.* Another set of important metrics, these measure how successful you are in your product adoption. This metric allows you to analyse which are the actual users that bring business value to your product.

- *Engagement.* This metric covers the number of users using your product, how they use each feature and how much time they spend during each task. This metric helps you separate your active users from less active ones, thus opening the way to building improvement strategies for both groups and increasing adoption.

- *Retention.* This metric will help you understand which users utilize the product consistently and which of them do not come back. It's essential to measure how many people go into the funnel vs out of the funnel. One thing to remember about retention metrics is that they 'do not provide enough color to be a complete management tool. As a result, many young companies overemphasize retention metrics and do not spend enough time going deep enough on the actual user experience. This generally results in a frantic numbers chase that does not end in a great product.'[7]

155

- *Monetization.* Probably a self-explanatory metric. It allows you to measure your product's revenue in terms of net revenue or revenue per user.

As you can imagine, mastering all of these high-level metrics can help your product in many ways, but one of them really stands out in the context of this book: *engagement.* Because our primary focus is on analytics specific to evaluating user experience rather than product analytics in general, we will concentrate our attention on product analytics that fall under it. One thing to keep in mind: no single metric is going to give you the full picture or a complete answer. Extracting insights from analytics is an art in itself. It takes lots of effort and experience to connect the dots and draw the right conclusions. It's also very different depending on the type of product, the industry and the context. For example, measuring user experience might be very different for a social media app and an internal enterprise tool, so it is important to select the right metrics.

Analytics for evaluating user experience

Data can be a powerful asset when evaluating the user experience of a product, but understanding that data isn't always the most straightforward task. When it comes to synthesizing product analytics, it pays to start by asking yourself some key questions: Is this metric important for this product and to your business? How does it compare with similar metrics? What trends are emerging from the data? etc. Answering these questions provides you with insights into how users interact with your product and allow you to use that data better to inform design decisions, fix usability issues or create new features. For this, we can use a variety of methods. I'm not going to list them all, of course (there are just too many of them), but I will detail and explain the ones that I think can help you the most in evaluating user experience as a designer, so make sure your product implements at least some of them:

- *Event tracking.* Perhaps one of the most important, because it will give you the base-level data. Collecting user activity, from clicks to page views and form submissions, can be accomplished through event tracking. As a result, this is one of the most sought-after tools in product analytics, but also one of the most misused. That happens because analysing event trends needs to be done by looking at more than one dimension of the user experience. Many product teams fail to understand that and make decisions based on two-dimensional data when in fact, they should look at multidimensional data. Especially when it comes to measuring user experience, two-dimensional analysis falls flat.

- *Funnel analysis.* This method is a powerful tool that offers insights into a user's journey through the experience by mapping out every step (for example, from user acquisition to revenue). It tracks users' activities at each stage, helping you understand how best to optimize your funnel for improved retention and higher conversion rates. It's also an essential tool to evaluate user experience as it quickly reveals drop-off points or usability bottlenecks. Although, in general, this type of analysis will not point you directly to the actual element that is hindering the user experience, it will give you a pretty good indication of what area you need to investigate.

- *Event mapping.* Event mapping creates a visual representation of user behaviour in a product by utilizing the actual screens as the canvas. There are various types that you will encounter in different tools, such as heat maps (showing areas with a high number of clicks/interactions), click maps (a sub-type of heat maps showing the exact location of each click) or scroll maps (displaying how much users scroll through a page and the areas of interest). These are usually used to identify usability issues or potentially improvements. A good example is a heat map or click map showing users clicking on a visual element that is not interactive – a very useful insight that you can use to inform your next iteration of the page.

- *Contextual surveys.* These allow you to get targeted feedback from your users. The main difference between these and a classic survey is that these get triggered by certain in-app events that you can control. This allows you to engage the user in a more direct way and, if done correctly, increases the chance of gathering useful data. They are usually very brief in nature (one to three questions) as they are meant for short, snappy, usually quantitative feedback.

- *A/B testing.* A very popular way of testing multiple design solutions for a specific area of your product to inform which variation performs better with your users. There's only one catch – the more A differs from B, the more the test becomes multivariate, so the results will be harder to interpret. For example, if you test two landing pages which have multiple different elements, such as titles, content, colours and call to action, it will be very difficult to assess which of these elements had more impact.

- *Session recordings.* These are essentially video recordings of user sessions. In a way, these are like running user testing sessions but with no goals, tasks or the ability to ask any questions. As opposed to classic user testing, you will be going in a bit 'blind'. Sometimes you might find it hard to understand why the user is going back and forth on a certain screen or using a feature in an unexpected way. It will give you some answers, but not all of them.

Just to wrap things up: as a UX designer, you can use analytics to make data-driven decisions that result in user experiences that are more tailored to the needs of your users. Tracking metrics allows you to get the pulse of the product, look at its performance, assess the efficacy of changes over time, and refine your overall user experience as needed. By using insights from product analytics to evaluate user experience, design teams are guaranteed greater chances of creating a delightful user experience.

Notes

1 J Nielsen. 10 usability heuristics for user interface design, 15 November 2020. NN/g, www.nngroup.com/articles/ten-usability-heuristics (archived at https://perma.cc/P7R6-LEEB)

2 J Nielsen. Jakob's Law of Internet User Experience, NNgroup, YouTube, 18 August 2017. youtube.com/watch?v=wzb4mK9DiHM (archived at https://perma.cc/WGS6-PKRC)

3 T Greever (2020) *Articulating Design Decisions: Communicate with stakeholders, keep your sanity, and deliver the best user experience*, 2nd edn, O'Reilly Media, Inc., Sebastopol, California

4 T Chamorro-Premuzic. Why you can't believe all the visual cues you get on video chats, FastCompany, 20 May 2020. www.fastcompany.com/90506857/why-you-cant-believe-all-the-visual-cues-you-get-on-video-chats (archived at https://perma.cc/VH5S-SEHM)

5 S Tardif. What every product manager needs to know about product analytics, Atlassian, nd. www.atlassian.com/agile/product-management/product-analytics (archived at https://perma.cc/A6LF-JA2A)

6 N Saini. 15 important product metrics you should be tracking, Amplitude, 9 August 2022. amplitude.com/blog/product-metrics-guide (archived at https://perma.cc/XR7B-Q9FB)

7 B Horowitz (2014) *The Hard Thing About Hard Things: Building a business when there are no easy answers*, HarperCollins, New York

CHAPTER NINE

UX strategy

I n this chapter we're going to talk about UX strategy. The term, when used broadly, can refer to multiple areas of UX, like the processes that designers use to build a successful roadmap, organizational processes showing how UX contributes to the design maturity of a company, or, perhaps at a lower level, what we can do in order for UX to be more impactful in relation to the business. In this chapter, I would like to focus more on the latter: how to be more effective in adding value with UX.

In today's digital world, a great user experience can be the backbone of your company's success. However, as we've discussed in this book so far, just creating an attractive interface isn't enough; you also need to design a UX strategy that caters to your user's needs, your business objectives and the product team's capabilities. Therefore, this chapter can be your guide for developing a strategic UX play that will bring value to your entire organization.

Balancing creativity and strategy

In the world of UX design, balancing creativity and strategy is essential for creating successful user experiences. While creativity is often associated by many with the artistic and aesthetic aspects of design, strategy is the backbone that ensures the product is aligned with the business goals and product objectives. In this section I want to show you why UX is not only a creative act but also a strategic initiative for your business. Designing a great user experience requires both. On the one hand, creativity is crucial for crafting an engaging, visually appealing interface that resonates with users. For a UX designer, it's the opportunity to ideate and experiment to come up with new and innovative solutions that result in pleasant user experiences. On the other hand, strategy is essential for ensuring that the design meets the business goals. For you as a designer, this will mean researching, planning, aligning teams and executing a plan to achieve measurable results. Creativity and strategy are very different, as you can imagine. You need to not only be able to execute both successfully but also switch between the two 'modes' quite frequently.

For you to create a successful user experience, it's essential to strike the right balance between creativity and strategy. But how do we do that? How do we balance what seems to be an artistic act with a more analytical act?

It has been suggested that 'Perhaps imagination is only intelligence having fun'.[1] So, why stop the fun at designing the user experience or the interface? Why not look at the entire process as an act of creation? Why can't strategy be creative? You see where I'm going with this. Yes, on a certain level, these two components are different, but if we look at the entire act of strategizing itself, it is, in essence, driven by creativity.

On multiple occasions, I've witnessed designers or other members of product teams compartmentalizing the two, separating what they think is their own area of expertise (the creative part of UX) and what they consider to be 'someone else's job'. Let me tell you why that's a bad idea, and if you want to be successful you need to treat both of them as a whole. Imagine you are working in a large company, designing a new and innovative product, and in the middle of a team debate around a specific UX solution, you start your argument with the infamous 'From a design perspective...'. Ok, what just happened now? I'll tell you what – you've lost the room because it's 'just another way of saying "from my perspective." Remember, we don't care about your perspective; we care about the user's perspective.'[2] Once you've done that, you've inadvertently disconnected yourself from both the users and the product and development team by essentially stating that you somehow 'represent' design, or the creative side. And you know what? By doing that, you've lost the ability to operate at a strategic level.

If you start separating the creative act from the strategic act, what you're doing, in reality, is devaluing what UX can do for the product and the business. You will be missing out on lots of opportunities to influence outcomes on both sides. Instead, what you need to do is allow creativity to transpire into every corner of your product. Do you think facilitating a stakeholder workshop can't be a creative effort? What about advocating for UX as a discipline in an organization that is not design-mature? Or perhaps building a long-lasting relationship with the engineering team so their focus on UX increases? See where I'm coming from? UX design isn't just about doing good research and creating nice user experiences. UX is also about being able to communicate and build bridges across disciplines, teams and cultures. Why would you give that away?

As you mature in your career as a UX designer, it will become more and more apparent that half of your job is to engage in conversations and build relationships. Your success as a UX designer will depend on how well you're able to do that. Even when working remotely, you will have to maintain relationships with the product team, engineering team, executives and other stakeholders. Being able to communicate clearly and effectively is essential. You will also need to be able to bridge the gap between disciplines and teams. You need to be the one who understands user needs, product requirements, engineering complexities and business objectives. To do all this, you need to learn to enjoy immersing yourself in productive, meaningful exchanges of ideas.

So, what does it take, in practice, to balance creativity and strategy in the context of user experience design and your day-to-day duties? Let me give you a few examples of things you can do or techniques you can use to become a natural at this:

- *Embrace storytelling.* You might ask yourself, 'Why are we starting with this? I'm a designer, not a writer!' But, are you not? Are you not a storyteller? I would argue that, for designers, storytelling is probably one of the most important skills they can have. For UX designers, in particular, it is *the* most important. Let me explain in simple terms: it does not matter how good your designs and ideas are if you cannot take your team with you on that journey. No amount of user research, design or testing can replace a good story. If you cannot get your ideas across to your stakeholders, anything you design is worthless because it's never going to get implemented, no matter how brilliant it might be. Is that starting to make more sense now? I genuinely hope so, because I encourage every designer I meet to work on this skill and never stop improving it. No matter at what level you are in your career, it will help you tremendously along the way. Storytelling will help you combine the creative side with the strategic side to deliver compelling reasons for your stakeholders to adopt your solutions. Good storytelling will eventually inspire your entire team and, as a result, make everyone more focused on what's important: having a good user experience.
- *Forge alliances.* Believe it or not, this one, too, is one of the most important aspects of the role. But what do I mean by

forging alliances? One thing you will learn while working with product teams is that not everything is as straightforward as it could be. It doesn't mean that if you gather business goals, user needs and technical requirements, everything is going to go smoothly. 'Even though everyone on the team is presumably working toward the same goal, often how to accomplish that goal can become a battlefield of differing opinions, each informed by the professional experience and expertise of their owners.'[3] So, there are always going to be bumps in the road. Maybe the business didn't communicate all its goals effectively, or maybe a product manager with a lot of influence has a different vision for the product, or maybe the engineering lead wants a different way of implementing the user experience. It's never going to be an easy ride. That is why forging alliances is key. Try to spend time with your key stakeholders and build up those relationships to a point where you feel that everyone's ideas are taken into account when it comes to decision-making. And since there are always going to be disagreements, having these alliances will make everything a lot easier.

- *Take people along on the journey.* If you want to create alignment within your team, there is only one efficient way to do that. Take everyone on the journey with you. That can mean anything from inviting stakeholders to your workshops to taking the time to synthesize and present your work to the wider team. Don't assume that just because you are doing great work, everyone else is going to understand that or even appreciate it. You make everyone part of the process, and you need to keep everyone in the loop. UX is the glue that keeps the team together.
- *Adapt, don't adopt.*[4] This one is more critical from a strategic point of view. As a UX designer joining a new organization, you will see that, at first, you will need to adjust your expectations to the realities on the ground. The new company might have different processes, a different way of doing things and potentially a completely new way of looking at UX design

as a discipline. However, I would encourage you to be a rebel at this point. Don't just blindly adopt every single process or way of doing things from your new job just because you want to please your new colleagues. Be analytical about it and see what works and what doesn't based on your knowledge and experience. Don't be afraid to adapt existing processes and propose new ways of doing things. Challenge the 'We've always done it this way' attitude, and long term you will have more to gain from this.[5]

- *Make everyone rave about UX.* When you become truly passionate about doing good UX, this will seems like a walk in the park. Before you know it, even without thinking about it, every little interaction with stakeholders or colleagues will become a way to evangelize UX because, let's face it, it is an exciting job. But before you get to that stage, you will need to start doing it consciously. Don't assume everyone should know what UX is or why it's valuable. So use every occasion to add some clarity to that. Of course, I don't mean explaining what UX is and does at every team meeting. This is more like sprinkling salt on a delicious meal. You need the salt for it to be tasty, but you should never overdo it because it ruins the entire dinner.

All in all, successful UX design merges creativity and strategy to drive the product and the business forward. For you, it's going to be essential to prioritize a user-centric approach, one that can ensure your designs meet both the user's needs as well as organizational goals and objectives. By using creative and strategic thinking together, you will be able to implement a more innovative yet efficient way of doing UX in your organization.

Stakeholder management

As you can imagine, stakeholder management is a key component when it comes to successful products. While it's easy to just focus on getting the design right, stakeholders can make or break your project if you don't get them on board (remember what I said in the previous section about forging alliances and taking people on the journey). UX design is collaborative by nature, and it will involve many stakeholders who will have different interests, goals and expectations. You need to learn this pretty early in your career because understanding how to manage stakeholders is an invaluable skill for a UX designer. It will help you navigate any number of complicated situations and ultimately achieve your goals. So next, we're going to go through a few techniques that can help you understand, prioritize and manage the expectations of different stakeholders to ensure the overall success of the product.

Stakeholder management techniques can be classified into four main types: engagement, communication, collaboration, and negotiation:

- *Engagement involves* interacting with stakeholders throughout the life cycle of the product through different activities like workshops and one-on-one meetings.
- *Communication* strategies involve ensuring there are clear lines of communication between all parties involved in the product, so everyone is kept up to date on progress and any changes.
- *Collaboration* strategies involve getting stakeholders involved in the decision-making process and making sure their opinion is taken into account seriously.
- *Negotiation* involves finding a compromise between stakeholders' goals and the needs of the users to reach a mutually beneficial outcome.

In terms of engagement, first and foremost, you should start with creating a stakeholder map, identifying all the stakeholders, their roles, interests and expectations in the design project. This quick and easy exercise will give you an idea of who you need to engage in what way, who you need to influence and who you need to keep informed. It is essentially a visualization of the balance of power in your product.[6]

Stakeholder mapping is a simple visualization of these circles of power within your product team. Using an onion skin type of visualization, you can map which stakeholders you need to monitor very close vs ones that you only need to keep informed. There are no golden rules to this, so every project will look different depending on many aspects, such as the type of product, the type and size of business you work in and even the industry where the product lives.

To begin, you will split this visualization into four main areas and map out the stakeholders according to each circle (Figure 9.1):

- *Manage closely.* This is your 'inner circle'. These are the *key* stakeholders that you want to keep as close as possible, taking them with you on the journey. Make them an integral part of your workshops and decision-making processes when it comes to design solutions. Good examples would be business, product and engineering stakeholders that need to be highly involved in the process.
- *Keep satisfied.* The second circle is dedicated to other important stakeholders that you need to always keep an eye on. Good examples are people from the marketing teams, legal, infrastructure and operations, finance.
- *Keep informed.* The third circle is for stakeholders that always need to be kept informed even if they are not very active within the product team. Depending on how your product is structured, these can be from various areas, similar to the second circle.
- *Monitor.* The fourth circle is for stakeholders that you need to monitor but not necessarily keep informed at all times. They include decision makers at a higher level who, even if they are not directly involved, may have a lot of influence.

Before we move forward, I want to clarify a couple of aspects in regard to stakeholder mapping. First, putting stakeholders into

FIGURE 9.1   Stakeholder mapping example

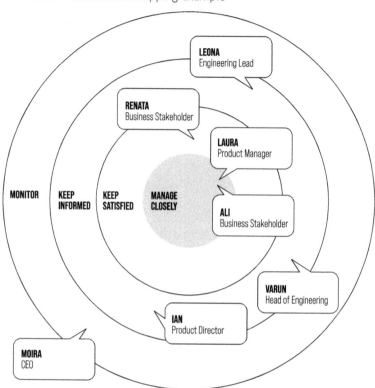

your closest circle of influence (one and two) doesn't mean the ones in circles three or four are less critical for the product, it just means they might not be actively involved all the time. A good example is the CEO role in a large organization. They would only be involved in the product development process in extremely rare cases, but that doesn't make them unimportant. In fact, they might be key decision-makers at critical moments in the lifetime of a product. So remember that, when it comes to stakeholder mapping, all circles are equally important. They are just different in terms of how much time you will have to dedicate to each of them. Second, keep in mind this mapping is not frozen in time. As you move along the product cycle, the map should change accordingly, with some stakeholders coming into your inner circle and others going to the outer circles. A good example of this is when you are about to hold a launch event, at which time marketing, legal and operations will ramp up their activity while others will ramp down.

In terms of communication, I've dedicated an entire section to this later on, but remember that communication doesn't need to be a fully formalized step that you need to take. You don't need to build an entire communication strategy, and you probably will not have the time to do it anyway unless you are part of a large design team working in a global organization, in which case it could make sense. All you need to do is sketch out a communication framework that outlines how the design team will communicate with stakeholders, what information will be shared, in what format and how often.

The following two areas, collaboration and negotiation, are closely related. That is because you can't have one without the other – they always go hand-in-hand. While collaboration takes care of the 'operational' part, mainly through conducting work-shops with the stakeholders to generate ideas, discuss solutions, and gather feedback, negotiation happens all of the time. Even if it's not immediately visible, every single interaction you will have with a stakeholder is a negotiation. As I said before, negotiation involves finding a compromise for a mutually beneficial outcome. This is done by taking into consideration every aspect of the product, from user needs to business goals to financial targets and overall company strategy. Compromise is, in many circumstances, a word with negative connotations, but in our case it doesn't necessarily mean this is a zero-sum game. It just means you are adjusting and accommodating to 'the needs of the many', which 'outweigh the needs of the few'. In case you were wondering, yes, I'm quoting from Star Trek – The Wrath of Khan, 1982.

Stakeholder management can be a challenging element of UX design, but it doesn't need to be complicated. Think about it this way: it's very much like managing a bank account. First, you need to monitor it regularly and see how much money you have left (just like establishing a baseline with your stakeholders). Then, you have to keep track of deposits and withdrawals. Think about these in terms of goodwill capital. Every time you make your stakeholder happy (by involving them in the process or sometimes by compromising on certain elements), you deposit to that account. Every time you need to challenge them, you withdraw from the account. You see where I'm going with this. Of course, this is by no means a scientific method, but as you gain more experience your instinct will be able to tell you how much you have left in that account.

Mastering communication

As a UX designer, you'll spend a lot of time speaking with stakeholders from all backgrounds – business, engineering, marketing, product, etc. To get your message across in a clear and concise manner, communication is key! But to become a great communicator, you first need to learn about the Turbo Encabulator. Yes, you've heard that right! Let me explain what this device is, and how can it help you master communication. Let's look at the definition first:

> The original machine has a base-plate of prefabulated aluminite, surmounted by a malleable logarithmic casing in such a way that the two main spurving bearings were in a direct line with the pentametric fan. The latter consisted simply of six hydrocoptic marzlevanes, so fitted to the ambifacient lunar waneshaft that side fumbling was effectively prevented. The main winding was of the normal lotus-o-delta type placed in panendermic semi-bovoid slots in the stator, every seventh conductor being connected by a non-reversible tremie pipe to the differential girdlespring on the 'up' end of the grammeters.[7]

I know, right? You're still in shock from reading this. Thankfully, the Turbo Encabulator is just satire, a fictional machine, though the description you've just read was indeed published by the British Institution of Electrical Engineers. What I do love about it is that it passes the test of time. Go to any stakeholder workshop or technical meeting these days, and it's close to impossible not to hear some technobabble. It always makes me think of the Turbo Encabulator.

But truth be told: this is what your stakeholders hear from you, and I know what you're going to say: 'No, I never use that kind of language.' Yes, you do, even if unconsciously. The sooner you realize it, the better. UX has a ton of jargon, and we've all been guilty of using it on occasion, so don't judge yourself too harshly. While the Turbo Encabulator is just an exaggeration, it's amazing at proving one point: *the way you communicate your ideas is critical.* So why do people still do it? I'm not going to go too deep into the psychology of it, but essentially it all comes down to insecurity. The work of many brilliant people goes almost unseen. This can happen for many reasons, but most of the time, it's just the nature of their particular role. For example, a back-end engineer's work is naturally less visible than a graphic designer's one. And so, members of the product team will try to emphasize their value in other ways. One of these ways is using a lot of jargon. By using lots of technical terms, many professionals hope to reveal the level of sophistication in their work. Needless to say, it never works that way.

At its core, good communication is about conveying complex ideas in a clear and simple way. This can prove difficult when dealing with stakeholders with different backgrounds, for example. Using lots of jargon and complex technical language will result in you losing the attention of the very people you're trying to persuade. On the other hand, effective communication skills will help you present your ideas in an accessible manner that everyone understands.

But let's see what you can actually do to improve this skill and make sure you get your ideas across to everyone in the team.

Here are my top tips for mastering good communication as a UX designer:

- *Listen.* I know, seems like an obvious one, but I need to repeat it. One of the most critical skills to have for effective communication is actively listening. As designers, you will need to listen carefully to your stakeholders and users to understand their needs and goals thoroughly. You can improve active listening by focusing your full attention, asking clarifying questions and repeating back what you have heard to ensure that you have understood correctly.
- *Speak the language of the room.* If you want to communicate effectively, there is nothing more important than speaking the language of your audience. As UX designers, you will need to communicate with stakeholders from diverse backgrounds and areas of expertise, such as developers, marketers and executives. Remember the Turbo Encabulator when communicating with these groups. Do yourself a favour and avoid using jargon and technical terms that they may not understand. It's not going to make you look smarter. Instead, use clear, simple and concise language that they can easily understand.
- *Use visuals* to strengthen your message. If you're a designer, it is likely that you are skilled at creating visuals to convey information. Now is the time to use this skill to your advantage. When presenting your ideas to stakeholders or users, use supporting visuals, such as icons, photos, wireframes and mock-ups, to help them immerse in the presentation and understand your thought process better. Don't be afraid to use visual metaphors
- *Use storytelling.* This is a powerful communication tool that can help you engage your audience. Don't just list your ideas in a dry and unemotional way. Take the audience on a journey for them to understand your rationale and your goals better.

Use storytelling techniques such as utilizing a narrative structure, focusing on emotions or using metaphors and analogies. This helps you connect emotionally with your audience and make your message more memorable.

- *Iterate and improve.* Finally, because UX is your speciality, make sure you iterate your communication work. Listen to feedback from your audience and go back and adjust your style and delivery method accordingly. What works in one situation might not work in another, so try to be as inquisitive as possible. Good communication requires practice and continuous improvement. Over time, developing this essential skill will help you more than you realize now.

When communicating with your line manager you can apply all these principles. I advise you also to use Andrea Picchi's Report–Decision–Support method. He explains in his book *Design Management* that you should prepare a list of things you want to discuss and label them as 'Report', 'Decision' or 'Support'. Report items are the ones that require a concise summary of the situation to keep your manager informed about deadlines, *Decision* items require your manager to commit to an action to move the workflow forward, and *Support* items need assistance from your manager.

By mastering communication skills, you can build strong relationships with your team members and all stakeholders involved in the project and be seen as an enabler when it comes to building bridges between disciplines and aligning objectives. All you have to do when going into your next presentation or workshop is to *leave your flux capacitor at home.*

Notes

1 G Scialabba. Mindplay, *Harvard Magazine*, 1984, 86–87, 19
2 T Greever (2020) *Articulating Design Decisions: Communicate with stakeholders, keep your sanity, and deliver the best user experience*, 2nd edn, O'Reilly Media, Inc., Sebastopol, California

3   L Buley (2013) *The User Experience Team of One: A research and design survival guide*, Rosenfeld Media, LLC, New York

4   B Burg. Adapt, don't adopt: How to learn from everyone but stay yourself, The Business Journals, 2 June 2016. www.bizjournals.com/bizjournals/how-to/growth-strategies/2016/06/how-to-learn-from-everyone-but-stay-yourself.html (archived at https://perma.cc/HW82-8BM4)

5   B Zimmerman. The most dangerous phrase in business: We've always done it this way, Forbes, 28 January 2019. www.forbes.com/sites/forbeslacouncil/2019/01/28/the-most-dangerous-phrase-in-business-weve-always-done-it-this-way (archived at https://perma.cc/C7GV-HXJW)

6   A Savina. Complete stakeholder mapping guide, Miro, nd. miro.com/blog/stakeholder-mapping (archived at https://perma.cc/K4SB-HXBV)

7   J H Quick. The Turbo-Encabulator in industry, *Students' Quarterly Journal*, 1944, 15 (58), 22

CHAPTER TEN

UX and product management

I'm dedicating an entire chapter to this topic because user experience and product management (PM) are two strongly interconnected disciplines. Understanding this early on will pay off later in your career, and it will have implications in regard to the quality of your design work. I'm going to go through similarities and differences, and highlight critical aspects of this relationship that can contribute to a successful product.

I'll also be sharing some practical tips and strategies for collaborating with product managers to help you nurture that connection and enable you to create exceptional products that truly resonate with your users.

Drawing the line between UX and PM

So, where do we draw the line between user experience and product management? This is a very hard question to answer because the tech industry is in a continuous state of evolution.

By that, I mean I would have probably answered this question in a different way five or ten years ago. To better understand where we can draw the line, let's see how two very influential product leaders of our times define product management:

> 'The job of a product manager is to discover *a product that is valuable, usable, and feasible*,' says Marty Cagan, Founding Partner of Silicon Valley Product Group and a 30-year veteran of product management. Similarly, our own Martin Eriksson calls product management *the intersection between business, user experience, and technology* (only a product manager would define themselves in a Venn diagram!).[1]

I love both these descriptions, but particularly Martin Eriksson's one because it mentions UX specifically, recognizing that a big part of a PM's role sits, in fact, under the user experience

FIGURE 10.1   Product management is at the intersection of business, user experience and technology

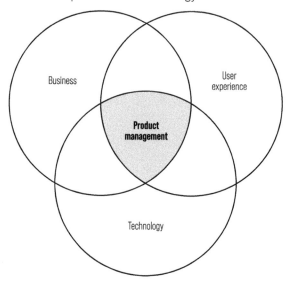

umbrella. In a more traditional sense, UX is focused on crafting user experiences by employing research and design methodologies that are meant to generate solutions which resonate with the target users. On the other hand, product management focuses more on product and business strategy, development and delivery of the actual solution. However, these distinctions aren't hard and fast. Clearly, there is an overlap between UX and PM. For example, a product manager might be responsible for guiding the design of new features or ensuring a good user experience when interacting with the product. Similarly, a UX designer might work closely with a product manager to gather business requirements or user research data that help shape the overall product strategy.

So again, where do we draw the line? The answer is within the question itself, and it might not be what you expect. The solution is that *we don't*. There is no need to draw a line between the two disciplines. The two have not only learned to co-exist but have formed a strong symbiosis, especially in the past decade when user-centricity has become a fundamental part of any successful product.

To illustrate this point better, I'm going to share what I recall about a fantastic conversation with one of the best product leaders I've ever had the pleasure of working with. The discussion started from the fact that even today there seem to be old expectations and misconceptions about what user experience as a discipline is supposed to bring to the product table. We both immediately thought about the elephant in the room – the *misconception* that UI alone is the same as user experience. For seasoned UX designers and product managers, this disheartening fallacy is not something new. Nevertheless, it keeps being perpetuated, and, to some degree, I've encountered it in every single company I worked with, regardless of the level of product and design maturity of the organization. So how can this be happening? Something doesn't add up. Partially it can be due to the fact that many product managers transitioned from project management roles (I'll touch upon this topic a bit later in this chapter), but still, this doesn't fully explain the problem. But the answer was staring us in the face. It's the UI! When you're not part of the process of designing a user experience, all you see in your mind is the final product. It's extremely hard for anyone to think about this abstract thing called UX when what they have in front of them is a nice, colourful interface. And then it clicked! We both worked on application programming interfaces (APIs) before, and we realized that we didn't encounter the same issue there. We both remembered how everyone in the team was intensely focused on designing the user experience. Prashant Agrawal, product manager at Postman, even states it: 'design APIs like we design user experience'.[2] The reason for that is when it comes to APIs, the user experience is far more critical than any user interface that we might build to serve the user. Simply put, the UI gets out of the way, and the entire team, no matter the role, is focused on the UX.

Obviously, a good UX-to-PM relationship begins with understanding each other's roles and responsibilities. Product managers should understand the various types of UX design methodologies available and how they can be used to design the best user experiences. By far the best product managers I've worked with were the ones who understood that UX research could give them the tools to make informed product decisions. Similarly, UX designers should have a good understanding of the product strategy, the roadmap and the resourcing available.

It's also important to recognize that in best-performing products, UX designers and product managers are far from being adversaries but rather partners in creating a great product experience. To lay the foundations for a strong partnership with your product manager and build a bridge between these two disciplines, I would like you to follow three simple rules:

- *Keep your product manager close.* Working closely with your product manager throughout the product development life cycle is essential for creating a successful product. This means going through each step of the process together to ensure that the product is meeting user needs, business goals and technical requirements. That's the technical part. But there is another facet to this. On a psychological level, once you work closely with someone on the same initiatives, the relationship changes from a transactional one to a partnership. Both are no longer concerned with how they will benefit individually but rather understand that, together, they can both achieve better results.

I'll give you an example: we all tend to have good days and not-so-good days at work. You've missed some important edge case in your designs, and the development team has flagged the issue in the daily stand-up. Imagine you could be in two scenarios: *scenario 1*, where you and your product manager are engaged in a purely transactional relationship, and *scenario 2*, where you are in a partnership. I'll ask you. Which scenario would you prefer? While scenario 1 does have some advantages, like having more autonomy, scenario 2 has something unique: it can give you the psychological safety you need, and that is key to a high-performance team. Just remember that this works both ways.

- *Protect your product manager.* This is related to my previous point. The job of a product manager can be very difficult at times. They are required to manage business expectations, budgets and delivery timelines while also focusing on user needs. That can be a lot to take in for anyone, and it's very easy to hit a bad patch. That is when you need to step in. As UX designers, you are a product manager's counterpart in the product team. Particularly when working within agile teams, there will be a lot of meetings that you're going to attend together. On many occasions, things tend to heat up. Pay attention and make sure you protect your product manager when necessary by adding context, extra information or simply aiding them in their effort to communicate with the team or with stakeholders. You will see that they will return the favour.

- *Connect on a daily basis.* Regular communication between UX designers and product managers is critical for maintaining a strong relationship. And I don't mean strictly talking about your product, but also sharing general insights, ideas and feedback that is relevant for both. This, in return, will build trust. Use these regular sessions to set expectations together. This could be for timelines, deliverables, design solutions or anything else that can help the product development process run smoothly. Personally, in my meetings with my PMs, before everything else, I ask a very important question: 'What's your top priority this week?'

When I describe the UX-to-PM relationship to the designers I'm mentoring, I usually give the example of an Olympic relay race. Each member of that team can never finish the race on their own, so the strategy is to use all their energy for a short period of time and pass the baton to the next person. Working with your product manager should be the same. For this to work perfectly, make sure you are there for them when they're trying to pass the baton to you.

Prioritization is king

You've finished your designs, completed the story mapping and created the user stories by working with your product manager and development team. But the question is: what to start working on first? What UX designer or product manager hasn't been there? Staring at a seemingly never-ending backlog of product features, wondering which ones to prioritize and why. But I have some good news: both UX and PM are all about setting priorities. While some elements are foundational and easier to prioritize, like setting up the infrastructure and working on them straight away, when it comes to product features things can get tricky. Depending on the MVP you've defined, you will need to consider a specific set of features to enable the user to perform their tasks.

The success of any product relies heavily on how effective the team can prioritize the work. Prioritization is the process of determining which tasks or features to work on first based on the needs of the users, business goals and available resources (budget and people). This is an essential practice you need to get familiar with in order to ensure the team focuses on what's most important. There are various frameworks out there that can help designers and product managers make these decisions in an easier way. My intention here is not to teach you how each of them works but rather how to think holistically and use any framework effectively. Remember what I said in previous chapters: any framework is better than no framework at all. But let's have a look at some popular ones that you will undoubtedly encounter in your career:

- *MoSCoW:* This technique involves categorizing tasks or features as must-haves, should-haves, could-haves, and won't-haves.
- *Kano model:* This framework involves categorizing tasks as basic needs (threshold attributes), performance needs (linear attributes), and delighters.
- *The Eisenhower matrix:* This technique involves categorizing tasks in a 4x4 matrix that contains urgent, important, not urgent and not important. If, for example, a task is deemed urgent and important you will need to start work on it right away.
- *Weighted shortest job first:* This framework involves prioritizing tasks based on calculating their cost of delay, job size and risks involved.
- *Impact–effort matrix:* This framework assigns tasks or features to one of four quadrants: big bets, quick wins, money pits and fill-ins.
- *Feasibility, desirability, and viability scorecard:* This is a framework developed by IDEO that scores items across three criteria of feasibility, desirability and viability, and ranks them based on the sum of individual scores.

As you can see, high level, these frameworks are all very similar. Each of them will provide you with a way to identify the most important tasks and decide in which order you need to get them done. However, each framework has its own nuances that may make it better suited for certain circumstances. Ultimately, you should familiarize yourself with all of them and choose the one that best fits your needs.

Having explored some prioritization techniques, let's now have a look at some important factors you need to consider when doing the actual prioritization exercises:

- *Involve stakeholders.* A prioritization session is only valid if all relevant stakeholders have a chance to participate. Make sure to include representatives from all areas of the product team: design, product, engineering and business.
- *Don't lose track of the product vision.* Sometimes, it's easy to get distracted by numbers, so make sure your prioritization is in line with your product vision at all times. This should guide any prioritization process regardless of the framework you choose.
- *Prioritize based on your team's limitations.* When prioritizing, take into account the skills and structure of your team. How many back-end developers do you have compared to front-end developers? Are they experienced enough? Does a certain feature require a special set of skills that maybe only one person in the team has? Take into consideration all other limiting factors, such as annual leave, public holidays, dependencies on other products etc.
- *Identify high-impact tasks.* Add more weight to the tasks that have the most significant impact on the product and the business.
- *Use data-driven metrics to make decisions.* Often, prioritization sessions will end up being very subjective based on the personal goals or ambitions of the stakeholders involved.

While it's not realistic to expect that you can remove all bias from the equation, you can do something to limit it. Using data to understand and inform your priorities is one way of doing this. This can be anything from qualitative user research data to quantitative data from usability testing, surveys or analytics.

- *Weight the evaluation criteria.* Not only can you use these frameworks to prioritize your backlog, but you can also use them to weight and prioritize the criteria you're going to use in the framework. A good example is the team deciding to put more weight on user feedback over stakeholder opinions.
- *Re-evaluate priorities.* I've mentioned this several times in the book, but let me state it again: things change, and they change quite rapidly when it comes to product development. These are usually events that are not under your control, like a competitor launching a similar product or feature, or your company cutting part of the budget. You will need to constantly re-evaluate your priorities and course-correct or pivot your efforts in a new direction.
- *Keep it simple.* Product teams tend to get lost in details or very technical discussions. To avoid that, make sure to use the best framework for your context. Spending more time explaining how the framework works instead of actually using it is a sign you're not doing things right.

By getting familiar with the right prioritization techniques and implementing them, UX designers and product managers can ensure the product backlog is an accurate reflection of the product vision and goals. Again, it's important to remember that product priorities can – and will – change over time, so be sure to keep run prioritization sessions frequently to keep up to date with any changes. And finally, don't forget to have some fun. Prioritization is a great opportunity to get together as a team and focus on achieving a common goal.

Project vs product

Ok, here we go. The infamous project vs product topic. In the product world, the terms 'project' and 'product' are frequently used interchangeably when describing at a high level the collaborative effort to build a piece of technology. While both share some similarities, they are not the same. Next, I will describe what the best-suited development methodology is for each of them, the differences and similarities between them, and some advice that UX designers or product managers might find valuable when dealing with these terms.

Most importantly, the main difference between a project and a product is the methodology they use. Projects use the waterfall methodology, which is a sequential, linear approach that is better suited for initiatives with a clear set of requirements and a defined timeline. A project involves several stages, such as planning, designing, developing, testing and deployment.[3] On the other hand, a product generally uses an agile methodology, which is a more flexible, iterative approach that is better suited to initiatives with an ongoing timeline and rapidly changing requirements. It involves a continuous cycle of researching, planning, designing, developing, testing and refining to achieve the desired product. As you can see, there is a significant difference in philosophy. One is more conservative and risk-averse, and the other is more flexible and open to change.

One important thing I want to mention: this is not a battle between old and new. Project management is not old-fashioned, and product management is not that new, either. What you need to remember is that both can be successful if properly managed and applied in the right context. Just don't go to an agile conference and mention the word 'waterfall'.

Table 10.1 is a side-by-side comparison of some of the differences and similarities between these two types of methodology, using multiple criteria.

TABLE 10.1   Project vs product: differences and similarities

Aspect	Project	Product
Methodology	*Waterfall*, which is a traditional project management approach that emphasizes planning and control, with a focus on completing each stage before moving on to the next. Waterfall is well suited to projects with a *clear set of requirements and a defined timeline.*	*Agile*, scrum, kanban, or other agile methodologies, which prioritize flexibility, collaboration and feedback. Agile approaches are well suited to products with an *ongoing timeline and rapidly changing requirements.*
Main Focus	Building a product that *meets specific requirements and objectives*, with a focus on delivering value to the client or stakeholder.	*Meeting user needs* or solving a problem, with a focus on delivering value to the end user and the business. Products are designed to enhance user experience and solve real-world problems, prioritizing long-term value add.
Type of Planning	*Predictive planning.* Projects typically require a comprehensive planning phase at the beginning of the project to define the requirements, scope, timeline and budget.	*Adaptive planning.* Products require ongoing planning and prioritization based on user feedback, market trends and business objectives. The planning process is iterative and incremental, with each iteration building on the previous one.

(continued)

TABLE 10.1   (Continued)

Aspect	Project	Product
Initiative Goals	*One-off delivery*, such as building an application, launching a marketing campaign, or completing the refurbishment of a building.	*Continuous improvement.* The goal is to meet the user's needs or solve a problem, such as a mobile app that helps people manage their finances, a product that simplifies daily tasks or a tool that enhances productivity.
Timeline	*Defined start and end dates*, with a focus on reaching specific milestones within the timeline. Projects often have tight deadlines and require close monitoring of progress to ensure timely completion.	*Ongoing timeline*, with a focus on continuous improvement and adaptation to changing user or business needs. Products evolve over time based on these aspects.
Approach	*Linear, sequential, and well-structured*, with a clear succession of phases, such as planning, designing, developing, testing and deployment.	*Iterative and incremental*, with a flexible and adaptable approach that allows for frequent adjustments. Products are developed through a continuous cycle of ideation, testing and refinement, with each iteration building on the previous one.

(*continued*)

TABLE 10.1   (Continued)

Aspect	Project	Product
Deliverables	*Specific set of deliverables* that need to be completed within the timeline, such as a website with specific features, a marketing campaign with specific objectives or a software system with specific functionality.	*Multiple deliverables that will iterate over time*, for example a mobile app that is updated with new features. Products are also developed in stages, with each stage delivering a specific set of features or improvements.
Resources Needed	People, technology, materials and budget allocated specifically for the project, with a focus on *maximizing efficiency and minimizing waste*. Projects require careful management of resources to ensure that they are used effectively to achieve the project objectives.	People, technology, materials and budget allocated specifically for the product, with a focus on maximizing user satisfaction. Products require *continuous review of the investment in resources* to ensure that they are competitive, relevant and sustainable over time.
Team	Typically involves a project team with a project manager, designers, developers, testers and other specialists who work together to complete the project.	Involves a product team with a product manager, UX designers, developers, testers, data analysts and other specialists who work together to improve the product over time.

(*continued*)

TABLE 10.1 (Continued)

Aspect	Project	Product
Scope	Normally has a *well-defined scope* with clear requirements, objectives and deliverables. The scope may be adjusted during the project as new information becomes available or priorities change.	Normally has a *broader scope* that may evolve over time based on user feedback, market trends and business objectives. The scope may be adjusted frequently to ensure that the product remains relevant and competitive.
Risks	Projects typically have a *higher level of risk* due to the tight deadlines, complex requirements and the potential for *cost overruns or scope creep*. Risks need to be identified and managed carefully throughout the project life cycle.	Products typically have a *lower level of risk* as they are *developed iteratively* over time based on user feedback and data analysis. Risks are identified and managed continuously throughout the product life cycle.
Metrics	Projects are typically *measured against specific metrics* such as budget, timeline and scope, with a focus on delivering the project within the agreed-upon parameters.	Products are typically *measured against user-centric metrics* such as customer satisfaction, retention, engagement and revenue growth, with a focus on delivering value to the end user and the business.

(*continued*)

TABLE 10.1   (Continued)

Aspect	Project	Product
Governance	Projects typically have a defined governance structure that includes stakeholders, sponsors and a project manager who is responsible for managing the project and ensuring that it aligns with the business objectives.	Products typically have a less formal governance structure that includes stakeholders, sponsors and a product manager who is responsible for ensuring that the product aligns with the business objectives and delivers value to the users.
Testing	Projects typically have a *dedicated testing phase* at the end of the project to ensure that the project meets the quality standards and requirements.	Products typically have *continuous testing and quality assurance* throughout the product life cycle to ensure that the product meets the user's needs and expectations.
Documentation	Projects typically require *comprehensive documentation* throughout the project life cycle, including project plans, requirements specifications, design documents, test plans and user manuals.	Products typically require *documentation that is focused on end-user needs and experience*, including user personas, user stories, user flows and design specifications. Documentation is developed iteratively and incrementally only when needed.

As a UX designer, you will, in most cases, work on products using the Agile mindset, but there will also be situations where you might need to work within a project team, so understanding the difference in approach and methodology will help you set the appropriate UX strategy for each. This will help you ensure that your team understands how user experience fits into the overall process and will inform decisions like when and what type of UX research needs to take place.

Notes

1 Mind the product. What is product management?, Mind the Product, nd. www.mindtheproduct.com/category/what-is-product-management (archived at https://perma.cc/SWB2-Q74V)

2 P Agrawal P (2019) Design APIs like you design user experience: Learn to design better APIs using concepts and processes which are used to design beautiful user experiences, Medium, 21 March 2019. medium.com/better-practices/design-apis-like-you-design-user-experience-a7adeb2ee90f (archived at https://perma.cc/NMT9-K24T)

3 ProjectManager. What is the waterfall methodology in project management? ProjectManager, nd. www.projectmanager.com/guides/waterfall-methodology (archived at https://perma.cc/U5PC-YXV3)

CHAPTER ELEVEN

UX tools

In UX design, using the right tools can often make a world of difference. Whether it's sketching out your ideas on paper or using sophisticated new applications to gather research insights, ideate or create high-fidelity prototypes, the tools that you choose to use can impact everything from how efficient your workflow is to the very quality of the final product. Choosing the right tool for the job can make your work life more enjoyable. But there's a challenge. With so many available tools on the market, it can be overwhelming to know where to start and which one to actually use. In this chapter we'll explore the different types of UX tools available to you, from user research and design to collaboration and data analysis. Whether you're just starting out in the field or are an experienced professional, this part of the book will give you a nice overview of the tools available to create the best possible user experiences. Let's begin!

You don't need any 'tools'

'Ok, what's going on here? You just told me UX tools are great.' I did, but there's a catch – for many designers who are just beginning their UX careers, there's the risk of falling in love with the tools. UX tools have evolved quite rapidly in the past few years, with some of them reaching impressive market shares. This was possible because those companies realized what the most important things designers needed from a tool were the ability to collaborate on, share and develop ideas. And they did this by designing amazing user experiences around those needs.

For experienced UX designers, these were not something new; on the contrary, this just mimicked the processes we've been utilizing for years. For new designers joining the UX field, however, it created a problem. The focus shifted from following the UX methodology to following the tool. This meant that an entire generation of designers were absorbed by the idea that they needed to focus their attention on a tool or a set of tools, rather than on UX methodology. Paul Adams, Chief Product Officer at Intercom, weighs in on this matter: 'designers certainly need to define the problem and solution not in pixels, but in terms of describing what happens between components in a system.'[1] It's likely that you have heard or read things like 'Ohh, you really need to try [product X]', 'If you're not using [product X], you don't know what you're doing', or, lately, '[Product X] is the industry standard.' What that does, is force you down a rabbit hole, one that will be hard to escape – *starting with the solution*. Unconsciously, you will jump ahead and not follow the process anymore. Once you've started using the tool, you're already working in the solution space. So what you should do instead, in the great words of Kaaren Hansen, Chief Design Officer at JPMorgan Chase & Co, is to 'fall in love with the problem, not the solution.'[2]

So, when I said you don't need any tools, I meant you should go back to the basics, start with the problem space and take it from there. At the heart of great UX design is human creativity – something which no application can replace. Don't lose sight of that. In fact, with a pen and paper, you can design the most amazing user experiences long before you even need to use a digital tool. Digital tools are there to help you bring your ideas to life, not to guide you to the solution. Therefore, don't be afraid to experiment with traditional methods. As long as you have a creative mind, pen and paper will be enough to develop great UX.

At this point, let's see when you actually *do* need the tools. UX tools are a great resource. They can help speed up your workflow, get better insights or design in a manner that's comparable to the real product. In short, UX tools are an extension of your own abilities.

In the next sections, I'm going to talk about some of the most-used UX tools that are available today and explain when is the right time to use them and how they can help you create awesome user experiences. From research to prototyping and testing, these tools should provide an excellent counterpart for your own skills.

User research tools

As you've learned earlier in this book, when we talk about user research, this can cover a rather broad area of expertise. UX research focuses on understanding the needs, goals and behaviours of our users. We can gather insights into these by using various methods such as user interviews, focus groups, usability testing, surveying or analytics. Obviously, I won't go into all of these, but rather I will pick and choose some popular ones that are available on the market at the time I'm writing this book. Again, my goal here isn't to recommend any specific tools but to give you some high-level understanding of when to use what type of tool.

User interview tools

This type of tool will help you with anything from recruiting your participants to organizing and recording the actual sessions and analysing the data. There are various ones on the market currently that partly cover this process. I am not aware of one single tool at this time that can handle the entire process without any real gaps. Let's look into some of them:

- *Zoom.* Perhaps you might find this surprising, but yes, Zoom is probably the top choice when it comes to user interview tooling. A reason for that is that many organizations have adopted it for their remote work and online meeting needs, which means you won't have to spend extra budget. But it's not all about the budget. It can handle well all your screen sharing and video recording needs and has some advanced features you will love, like recording to the cloud and automatic transcripts. A downside of Zoom is that it's less suitable to be used for in-person interviews, but it still does the job.
- *Calendly.* A very popular platform for scheduling meetings that can be easily repurposed for user interviews. It can integrate with multiple calendars, like Outlook, Google Calendar or Apple Calendar and allows us to save a ton of time by sharing available calendar slots with potential participants, who can then book the interviews at their convenience.
- *UserZoom, UserTesting, Dscout.* These platforms offer to handle the entire end-to-end process in one place. In my experience that's not really possible, because of how complex various user research techniques can be, but they are all very good choices if you prefer to use fewer tools in exchange for a bit less control.

Usability testing tools

As you've learned in this book, usability testing is a very important part of UX and user research. It allows you to test and get feedback on your designs, allowing you to de-risk your product before your designs get handed over to the development team. Let's see a few examples:

- *Maze.* A dedicated usability testing platform that has some very innovative features, such as direct integration with major design platforms, allowing you to pull in designs directly from your files. With Maze, you can perform various methods like task analysis, heat maps, A/B testing and many more.
- *Userlytics.* Another comprehensive user research platform that has a big focus on usability testing. It also has some very unique features like VR testing and sentiment analysis.
- *Loop11.* Another good option on the market currently is Loop11, a dedicated usability testing platform that offers its own unique features like information architecture testing, benchmarking and true intent studies.

Survey tools

There are countless options on the market when it comes to surveys, from options like Google Forms or Microsoft Forms that 'come with the package' to dedicated surveying platforms like SurveyMonkey, Typeform and AskNicely. Depending on your needs in terms of in-built logic, sharing, user experience and analysing the data post-study, based on my experience, the best choice is to alternate between them.

Analytics tools

Another very busy area of the market with countless tools on offer. In this category, I would like to mention a few that stand out from the rest by having innovative or unique features.

- *CrazyEgg, HotJar, Mouseflow and Smartlook.* I'm putting all of these in the same 'bucket' because they all have very similar features like the ability to see heat maps, record user sessions, check conversion funnels, etc.

Design and prototyping tools

When it comes to design and prototyping tools, you're only going to hear one name spoken by everyone, and that is Figma. Figma has managed to increase exponentially in popularity over the last few years, taking the reins from another very popular tool, Sketch. Both currently own a majority share of the market, with other tools like Axure coming a significant distance behind.

Simply put, Figma is a cloud-based design tool that enables UX designers to create and collaborate on user interfaces, prototypes and designs in real time. Figma offers some very innovative features, like the ability to collaborate live on a design, hand over the designs to the development team and create basic prototypes, all in one integrated tool.

The popularity of Figma is mainly due to the fact that it offers one of the most comprehensive ways to design user interfaces that does not compromise on its own user experience. As a result, it gained massive popularity among UI designers, and UX designers as well. One of the main advantages of Figma is that it's a cloud-based solution, meaning that designers can now work on projects from anywhere, on any device, without the need to download or install any software.

Another reason why Figma occupies the number one spot is the fact that it offers one of the most robust design system management capabilities with enterprise features, allowing designers to create and maintain design systems that can be shared across projects or even entire organizations. This is particularly important in large organizations with big design teams where many people can contribute to the maintenance of the design system.

Despite its popularity, Figma isn't necessarily the best choice for all UX designers. In fact, many designers in the UX community argue that because Figma only has basic prototyping capabilities, we cannot class it as a prototyping tool and that it remains just a very good UI design tool. Of course, there are nuances to this, for instance the complexity of your design. If, for example, you're just testing a design with some simple interactions and not very complex logic, Figma can very well do the job. However, if, for instance, you're working on a financial application, the data and the logic of the interactions become far more important than just the look and feel of the user interface. Luckily the market also provides for this; enter Axure.

Axure is probably the most powerful tool on the market when it comes to prototyping user interfaces. With Axure, designers can create complex interactions, animations and conditional logic, which can be very useful when working and testing on more complex projects, as I mentioned earlier.

When it comes to design and prototyping tools, most will end up choosing between Figma and Axure, but there's no right or wrong choice here. Both tools have their strengths and weaknesses, and the choice ultimately comes down to the product's needs. Figma is a great choice for designers who prioritize collaboration, while Axure is a better option for those who need more powerful prototyping capabilities and greater flexibility for usability testing. If you don't want to compromise on either of these, I have some good news for you – Axure built an integration with Figma, so it's now possible to work across these two platforms.

Collaboration and conceptualization tools

Collaboration tools are critical for UX in the context of today's world. In a business environment where companies have made hybrid working the norm, having access to online collaboration tools is not only desirable but a must. There are many collaborative tools on the market, but again, two stand out at a distance from the rest: Miro and Mural. Both these tools have very similar functionality, allowing users to access a digital whiteboard where they can collaborate with other people. In the context of UX design, this enables us to run design thinking sessions, stakeholder workshops and prioritization sessions remotely.

To explain how this works, I'm going to take Miro as an example. Similar to Figma, Miro is a cloud-based tool, which means you can access it on any device or operating system. Miro enables collaboration and conceptualization, which allow teams to work together in real time to create and share ideas. The platform provides a digital canvas or whiteboard that can be used to create posted notes, diagrams, mind maps, user stories, flowcharts, wireframes and other visual representations of ideas and concepts. Miro's user interface is very intuitive and easy to use, allowing team members to quickly create, edit and share content even when the meeting is being done remotely, enabling people to collaborate effectively.

One big advantage of collaboration tools is that they integrate with a wide range of other platforms, like Slack, Jira, Google Drive, Dropbox, etc. These integrations make it easy for people to bring content from other tools into tools like Miro or Mural and vice versa.

Data analysis tools

In this section I will touch upon data analysis tools for user experience design. As you've learned earlier in the book, performing user research or usability tests is just half of the work. It's equally important to be able to analyse that data and extract valuable insights to help us improve the user experience. Using dedicated data analysis tools will offer you several advantages over manual data analysis. Let's look at some of those advantages:

- *They save time.* Dedicated tools can help you analyse and interpret data quickly, which can save a lot of time compared to doing a manual analysis.

- *Accuracy.* Using data analysis tools helps to eliminate errors and inconsistencies that may occur during manual analysis, resulting in better insights.
- *Visualization.* Remember when we talked about visualizing your data to extract better insights? This is a key advantage of using dedicated data analysis tools. These offer various visualization options such as charts, graphs and tables, making it easier to understand and communicate these insights.
- *Automation.* This one is pretty straightforward. Automating anything from data cleansing to tagging or scoring data points can significantly increase your productivity, saving time and effort.

Remember when we talked about the importance of data-driven UX in Chapter 6? Let's look at what type of tools we need to perform data analysis for UX efficiently. There are various tools on the market that can do really well when it comes to either quantitative or qualitative data analysis. For quantitative data, there is nothing more popular than Excel. Basically, the entire world runs on Excel. From the banking industry all the way down to the corner shop, everything runs on Excel. Why couldn't we use it for UX as well? I can't say the same for qualitative data analysis. There, the landscape is much denser, and there are a plethora of tools available to choose from, such as MAXQDA and NVivo.

While dedicated tools do a great job, when it comes to data analysis for UX I prefer tools that are highly versatile and, ideally, can help us do both quantitative and qualitative analysis. One of my favourites in this category is Airtable.

Airtable is a cloud-based database and data analyses tool that combines the functionality of spreadsheets, databases and project management into a single platform. Or, as I also like to call it 'Excel on steroids'. Airtable will allow you to create data-bases, tables and fields, similar to a spreadsheet. However, the main difference is Airtable offers more advanced features such as cross-linking tables, grouping and sorting data, tagging data and filtering data. All amazing features for analysing both quantitative and qualitative data for UX. Another thing I really like about Airtable is the fact that you can automate a lot of the work. You can essentially use it all the way from recruiting participants for your study to sending thank-you emails post study.

New UX tools are being developed every day. The best way to stay up to date is to use social media platforms like Twitter, LinkedIn or Facebook, where you can follow UX communities or design influencers and stay informed about upcoming tools and trends. Once you've identified a tool you like, be sure to check trial versions or free versions of that tool and see how it can improve your workflow and design process even before it becomes popular.

In the end, UX is much more than the tools you use, it's about understanding the user. The tools are just a means to an end, a way to bring your design to life. What truly matters is the quality of the experience you create and the impact it has on the people who will use it.

Notes

1   P Adams. The dribbblisation of design, Intercom, 18 September 2023. www.intercom.com/blog/the-dribbblisation-of-design (archived at https://perma.cc/5Q37-SLT7)

2   J Jackson. Compassion is the key to innovation, Forbes, 9 February 2022. www.forbes.com/sites/jarretjackson/2022/02/09/compassion-is-the-key-to-innovation (archived at https://perma.cc/JR7G-HUW5)

PART THREE

How to become a UX designer

In today's increasingly digital world, user experience has emerged as an essential component of any successful product or business strategy. UX designers play a vital role in creating products that are not only visually appealing but also intuitive and user-friendly. In 2017 Jakob Nielsen of NN/g predicted that 'the UX profession is expected to grow from the current about 1 million people to about 100 million people' by 2050. This is not necessarily because everyone will be a UX designer by then, but because the more digitally enabled our world becomes, the more UX will transcend its current form and reach full-scale adoption. I imagine a world where UX will be taught in schools as the discipline of designing for everyday human needs, even beyond digital.

As the demand for UX designers continues to grow, many of you will be looking to pursue a career in this exciting and ever-changing field. I wrote this part of the book as your guide to building up a career as a UX designer, starting from the basics all the way to managing your career progression. For those of you who are not necessarily looking to become a UX designer but instead looking to hire one, this part of the book will help you understand what skills you need to be looking for and what type of people will be most successful in this job.

So, let's dive in and uncover the secrets of a UX career.

CHAPTER TWELVE

Getting started with UX

I always get slightly melancholic when I'm talking with young designers who are just about to break into the industry. In many ways, that's because it's also my story, and I get to re-live all the happy moments and challenges I faced. All I can say to those who haven't officially begun their UX career yet is that this is probably one of the most exciting and fun jobs you can have. You will get to meet a ton of people from all walks of life, and you'll never find yourself getting bored again. That, I can guarantee.

This journey has a lot of learning ahead, but hopefully this book will help you understand what to focus on first. I remember when I was first starting out, after a few months of avidly reading, trialling a few tools and, in general, trying to figure out the discipline, one day I became painfully aware of the vastness of the UX field. There were so many things that I knew contributed to UX that I even started to tell myself: 'Maybe this is not for you, I don't think you can make it. It's just too much to learn, and you're too late.' Looking back now, I can say that was probably

FIGURE 12.1   The Dunning-Kruger effect as a funny graph

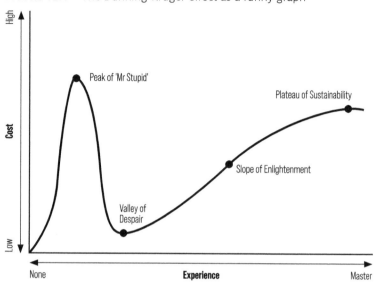

the moment when I, without even knowing it at the time, offi-cially became a UX designer. This was my silent Dunning-Kruger moment, finding myself in the 'valley of despair'.

I'm an avid consumer of internet memes. I think they capture the essence of communication, and on this topic there is a series of memes circulating based on the Dunning-Kruger effect. I particularly enjoy the one in Figure 12.1. It's by no means scientific, but based on my anecdotal experience coaching many aspiring designers it's actually 100 per cent true. Your career as a UX designer is likely to feel like that. Once you've found your-self in the valley of despair – and *you will*, trust me – you can, without a doubt, call yourself a UX designer.

And fear not, experiencing the valley of despair is a good thing. Jonathan Jarry (Science Communicator with the McGill Office for Science and Society) interviewed Dr Dunning on this topic for one of his articles, and this is what he had to say: 'The effect is about us, not them… The lesson of the effect was always about how we should be humble and cautious about ourselves.'[1]

So, lesson number one is be humble when it comes to learning about a complex topic. True knowledge only comes with time and experience.

Connecting the dots

Do you remember Steve Jobs' comment from Chapter 1 about connecting the dots looking backwards? Well, it's time to put that into practice for your future career, so please keep those words in mind whilst we go through this section.

As I mentioned before, in a way, this is also my story, so I want to share with you how the dots connected for me. I grew up in a small city in south-eastern Europe, in the northern part of Romania. Ever since I was a child, I've enjoyed playing with pencils and crayons. I have this very clear memory in my head from when I was maybe three or four years old, sitting one summer on the veranda at my grandma's house, watching the cars go by and recording the colour of each passing car on a notebook by drawing a coloured dot. After doing so for a few days, I noticed more cars were white as opposed to any other colour. So, because I was curious, I picked up my notebook and took my findings to grandma, showing her my dotted pages and asking her why more cars are white. Needless to say, I got one of the warmest hugs of my life and a satisfying response: apparently, white paint was cheaper, or so she thought. I smile when I think about this, as it was probably my first piece of research.

Fast forward to my final high-school year. I was working on my computer analyst diploma project, and my topic was a wiki website about PC components. Because I wanted a good grade, I watched what other colleagues were doing: websites with lots of news ticker text, vibrant colour buttons, HTML tables, background music and sparkling animated 3D letters. I know, crazy times, right? And in this primordial soup of design elements, I had an idea: instead of using all these ugly elements, why not use pictures of a PC and each of its components and explain it in a friendly, visual way? You would click on an element from the image and zoom in on the respective component. Enter the scene – HTML image maps. It was 20 years ago, ok? Don't judge! Obviously, I built the website and got my good grade with a design that resonated with everyone. It was just a school project, but it made me fall in love with digital design and creating user experiences.

I went on to study computer engineering for the next five years, and even though I did enjoy it a lot, I was starting to miss the creative challenges design gave me. Interestingly enough, life has a way of opening doors for you. Sometimes they're not exactly the ones you would expect, and in my first year after university I got a job as a computer store sales assistant. I would advise people on what PC to buy and with what configuration, based on their budget and needs. Not exactly the most inspiring job, but it helped me learn a lot about understanding client needs and running a small business. Since my thirst for creativity was still there, another door opened, again an unexpected one. I took a job as an architectural designer, and I stayed in the industry for the next five years. I was back in the game! It is a fantastic feeling working on design concepts, and then architectural plans, to later see them taking shape in reality.

You see, I would lie if I said I had planned my career, but the dots still connected with each other in my future. I think a career can't actually be planned in detail because many aspects that influence it will be completely out of your control. This is why many people 'accidentally' become UX designers. Some become great ones. With that being said, you should still have a career North Star. By that I mean having some outlying target that you want to reach in your future. If you don't set any goals for yourself it's much harder, if not impossible, to connect the dots later.

Each of the events I have recounted was a pivotal moment in time for me. If you think about it, without even one of them happening, my career would have looked entirely different. This is the butterfly effect in action. For example, if I had never worked in architecture, I would have never realized how similar it is to user experience design. In fact, in many of my conversations today with architects, I like to refer to architecture as 'UX for buildings'. And if you think about it, drawing parallels between architecture and today's digital product world makes so much sense. We have 'architects'(designers) that create the plans and sometimes design 'wireframes', we have 'developers' that 'build' projects, and we all care about 'usability', 'accessibility' and 'quality assurance'. As they say – there is nothing new under the sun. Use your knowledge today as a base for your future knowledge.

What I would like you to take away from this is the fact that every experience in your life can shape your career in one way or another. What you need to do is recognize the dots that matter because those will be the ones connecting and defining your future. I'm telling you all this based on my experience mentoring many junior designers. It's completely normal to feel insecure about not knowing how everything works or fits together today. The fact that the best UX designers I've met come from entirely different fields should give you a lot more confidence in your future.

Due to how vast UX is as a discipline, it's very common for UX designers to transition from other related disciplines like graphic design, engineering, computer science, architecture or psychology, but what I want to say is – it doesn't matter what field you come from. I'm willing to bet there is going to be a strong link to UX. And I know what you're going to say: 'Yes Adrian, but those are mostly technical fields, and I studied literature.' And my response will be the same one I give to the designers I'm mentoring: it doesn't matter! In fact, some of the best people I have ever worked with in the field never even studied technology-related subjects. For example, the best user researcher I ever met was a bartender before going into UX. Knowing how to talk to people made her not only well positioned to do user research interviews, but she was able to extract insights from users in a way that no one else could. You see where I'm going with this. Your background is less important, and having a different perspective can, in fact, be an advantage: 'Many people make their way to user experience by crossing over from an adjacent field. These crossovers are the people who are carrying UX forward, taking it to new levels and new organizations.'[2] UX is ever-evolving, so why should we stop doing that? I've met UX designers coming from all walks of life. What is important is your love for problem-solving, human behaviour and analytical thinking. Everything else you will learn in due course.

UX is, by nature, a truly interdisciplinary field. 'Studying' UX means that you will need to actually get familiar with multiple other disciplines like psychology, design, engineering, management, writing, etc. The chance of you having a skill that fits into any of those is actually very high. I keep going back to the connecting the dots metaphor. You will not be able to do it by looking forward, so instead, look backwards into your past and try to focus on things you love to do *today*. Things that don't necessarily feel like work to you but you enjoy doing and spending time on. Those are probably the dots you are looking for. If, in some cases, you feel 'no way could this have something to do with UX', don't! It will make more sense later.

But how does this work in practice? Let me explain. Say, for example, you are currently working as a sales assistant in a fashion store. You also have videography as a passion, and in your spare time you film interesting characters with amazing stories to tell, perhaps hoping to create a documentary one day. However, UX sounds exciting to you because you've always had this natural inclination towards technology and making new things. You also want to do better in terms of money, nothing wrong with that. None of this has anything to do with UX, right? You couldn't be more wrong! Now is the time to acknowledge your skills and start connecting some of those dots. Look backwards, what do you see? You have lots of experience dealing with people every day, some of them difficult to please. You know how to calm them down and make them leave the store happy. This means you already have two exceptional skills: empathy and negotiation. You will be a natural at interviewing people, finding out what their needs are and extracting those insights. You are also likely to be very good at managing stakeholders' expectations. And your videography skills in UX? Priceless. You will know how to set up camera angles and the best way to capture gestures and reactions. You will be able to edit your videos and present snapshots to the team. This is what I'm trying to say. Look backwards, and connect the dots!

So, if you consider yourself ready to give UX a chance, that is your starting point. Sit down and think about your best skills on the one hand and the things that make you happy on the other. *Your strongest skills and the things you enjoy doing* will be your entry point into the industry. All you need to do is capitalize on those and start building your UX story from there.

Navigating an ocean of job tiles

UX designer, product designer, UX/UI designer, visual designer, UI designer, user interface designer, interaction designer, UX architect, UX researcher, UX engineer, UX designer engineer, UX developer, UX/UI developer, UX strategist, business designer, experience designer, user experience designer, application designer, UI artist, creative technologist, digital designer, user journey specialist, UX/product designer, UX designer engineer, service UX designer, product developer, digital UX/UI designer.

These are all real job titles related to UX that I just gathered from LinkedIn. I know what you're going to say: 'This is crazy!' and I can't blame you for it. I imagine how you feel, on the other side, trying to navigate all of this. You must have a ton of questions. Besides worrying about how to break into the industry, you now also have to worry about what these job titles mean and which one you should apply for.

For an industry that is supposed to be about clarity, we've really messed this up, haven't we? So how did we get here? The answer to that is pretty simple. Historically, managers who were in charge of hiring UX designers didn't have a background in UX themselves, so they started to write job descriptions according to their own needs and interpretations of what the role should entail. Take, for example, the infamous and unnecessary title of 'UX/UI designer'. How did this one come to be? As managers looked to scale design across their organizations in a cost-efficient way, they became painfully aware of the fact that very few people can do everything UX, from research to delivering high-quality UI and prototypes. So this was their way of saying: 'We're looking for someone who can execute the entire process end-to-end', which is less realistic, of course. And this is how the unicorn or the 'UX team of one' was born. A mythical creature that can do everything UX. Has creating a new job title helped with this? Has this magically created more talented designers? Of course not. Many specialized UI designers just changed their titles to UX/UI, creating a huge reshuffle in the industry among people who could do the visual part very well but had little experience with UX methodology. And transitioning isn't the problem here. I'm a big supporter of career shifts, having done it myself. However, skipping essential steps in the process is a problem. My advice? Make sure you don't forget to learn the skills. Overall, this quick, artificial shift of skipping the learning process and transitioning directly just by changing the job title devalued UX as a practice, because instead of having to do months and months of learning you could just change your title, right? What could possibly go wrong?

What I want you to understand is one thing: job titles don't actually matter. Yes, you've heard that right. Here's the truth: with a few small exceptions (like UX researcher, UX writer or UI designer, which are highly focused on a particular niche), you could probably put all of the titles listed at the start of this section under the same umbrella: 'UX designer'. What's important is that you work to gain the skills and experience needed to do the job. A 'UX designer' may sound different from an 'interaction designer', but both roles require pretty much the same strong knowledge of user-centred design principles, and the same processes and methodologies. The reason why so many titles are still being used (and we're probably still creating new ones as we speak) is that most organizations are not design mature, and they are trying to compensate for the lack of knowledge on how to scale design through creating highly specialized niche titles according to their current needs. As you can imagine, this hasn't helped them get better people on board, so slowly this practice has been reversing. Organizations started to understand that role in itself is still that of a UX designer.

As you start doing more research into the field, you will start encountering lots of terms like the 'T-shaped UX designer'[3] or even the 'M-shaped UX designer', which is essentially a fancy way of describing 'people who have *depth of skill and experience in one discipline*, represented by the vertical stroke, while also having breadth via skills and experience across other disciplines, represented by the horizontal stroke.'[4] Your takeaway from this should be simple: you need to strive to become a T- or maybe M-shaped designer. Where those lines are drawn will depend on your skills and the things you enjoy working on.

Keep in mind that you should not focus at all on job titles. Instead, focus on becoming a well-rounded UX designer. For that, it's important to start by listing your passions and identifying areas where you have already developed your skills, as well as areas where you need to study and learn new skills. Once you have identified these, it's essential to plan how to acquire the knowledge you need and to dedicate consistent time and effort towards these learning goals.

You will find the field of UX to be dynamic and exciting, and it's easy to get caught up in the latest trends and buzzwords. My advice for you is to always go back to the basics; the core principles of user-centred design have not changed over time. Keep these principles at the heart of everything you do, and you will be successful, no matter what your job title may be. Last but not least, don't be afraid to fail. We do most of our learning through failing at different things. Go out and get the job you dream of!

A beginner's guide to the industry

In this section I would like to give aspiring designers some practical advice on how to break into the industry. And don't worry, even if you're well into your UX career or reading this book for any other reason, the advice I'll share here will prove to be very useful.

So, without further ado, here are my top recommendations for when it comes to starting out in UX.

Start small by building your UX skills and knowledge

As I've mentioned several times in this book, UX design is a vast discipline that encompasses many different areas, such as UX research, UX strategy, interaction design, UX writing, etc. When you first begin, you are likely to feel overwhelmed by the complexity and the sheer amount of information that will hit you. Don't panic, and definitely don't quit! It's perfectly normal to feel that way. This will only get better over time. Based on my anecdotal experience, it takes someone that is completely new to UX one to two years to get comfortable with the discipline, maybe less if you already come from a related field. When I say 'getting comfortable', it doesn't mean you will know all the ins and outs of UX. Related to this, I remember having this amazing professor at the university who told us (and I'm paraphrasing): 'As an engineer, you don't need to know all the answers, what you need to know is *where to look for the answer.*' This means that you will reach a point in time when you will have enough knowledge to search for the answer by yourself, confidently. To make it easier, start with an area that interests you the most, work on developing the relevant skill set and then expand from there. This will be different for everyone, depending on many factors like previous experience, career goals or passions. Some people will start with research, others with interface design, and so on. The way in which you approach UX doesn't really matter. In fact, just by reading this book right now you will hopefully have a much clearer idea of what you need to work on first.

Get a mentor early on

Don't wait until you become a senior designer to get a mentor. In fact, I should use the plural 'mentors', as one will not be enough. Don't shy away from contacting experienced designers and asking them to mentor you in your new career. Many will be happy to do it free of charge, and it will help boost your confidence tremendously. Not only that, but try to think of having mentors like being able to access secret doors. On many occasions, a mentor can save you lots of headaches and get you focused on the things that matter the most. This is not cutting corners! This is using someone's previous experience to your advantage. It's also not uncommon to get mentors from related or completely different disciplines. I personally had mentors with backgrounds in architecture, engineering, product management, psychology, arts, etc. Each of them had something valuable to contribute to my career. Some mentors will give you technical advice, others will give you advice on interpersonal skills or leadership. Be sure to take it all in and learn from it. The design leader Andrea Picchi supports this approach and advocates for the creation of what he calls a 'board of mentors': 'Having your board of mentors composed of subject matter experts on critical areas for your professional development can profoundly impact your career trajectory, augmenting your abilities during challenging moments and propelling your growth to a level otherwise unattainable. Creating a board of mentors requires time, effort and opportunities and therefore should be considered a priority early in your career.'[5]

You don't need a job to practise UX

Many aspiring designers will struggle to get into their first job. Don't make the mistake of thinking that you need that job to be able to learn UX. Some people enter this vicious circle and end up quitting because of it. Taking courses, reading books and talking to like-minded people all have no real value if you don't actually get your hands dirty and start practising your skills on real projects to build up your portfolio. I'm going to repeat that so it's very clear: 'on real projects'.

A big problem I see today is with people coming from various design schools and UX boot camps. The majority of them haven't worked on real projects, and you can immediately see it in their portfolios or the way they talk about UX. They talk the talk but can't walk the walk. I have nothing against rapid learning, and I think particularly UX boot camps have done a great job of bringing more people into the discipline. However, I think they've also failed in one regard. In an effort to scale their businesses to more students, they had to use what they call 'practice projects', which are nothing more than fictional products that their students will practise on. The problem with this is that it instils false expectations for what UX is and creates a 'design in a bubble' mindset. If you're working on a fictional product, no matter how cool it sounds, everything around it will be just that: fictional. Fictional users with fictional needs, fictional business goals and a fictional delivery of the product. In fact, in most design schools or boot camps UX design stops with the prototype, if you even get to that stage. There is a huge part of UX that's being left out – implementing the design. This creates bad habits, which is something you should avoid at all cost. My advice here is simple: no matter how cool that fictional product looks like, a real project is worth ten times more. You will get exposure to real-world problems and interact with real users and stakeholders.

I know what you're going to say: 'But it's hard to find a real project to work on when I don't even have a job.' Let me tell you, it's easier than you might think. There are multiple ways to do UX without having a job. For example, you can apply to work for a non-profit organization, which will expose you to real projects, and also you'll get a chance to do some good. Win–win. If that doesn't work, find small local shops or companies that you like that are in desperate need of design. Redesign their website or app pro bono. In many cases you will end up forming lasting relationships with them and may even get paid. Alternatively, design something real for yourself. Maybe you want to start a design community where designers starting in the field can collaborate and share learning. You'll need a website or an app. You see what I'm getting at. Any amount of real-world experience is better than fictional work or no work, and trust me when I say this, it's going to help you at your interviewing stage.

Learn to use networking

Often overlooked, this is a must for designers that are just beginning in the industry. Attending industry events, joining design communities and conferences, or even reaching out to people in the field to interview them for an article you're writing are all very good ways to build connections and relationships that can later help you learn more about specific jobs or find new and exciting opportunities. You never know what doors might open by simply talking to people. In time, this will also increase your confidence levels, as you will be more comfortable with interacting with bigger groups of people or more senior stakeholders. Make networking a habit and it will pay off in the long run.

Don't get too hung up on titles, and be willing to start small

When you first begin your journey into UX, remember that job titles can be subjective and can vary widely between companies. Job titles, in most cases, are a reflection of organizational structure and culture rather than a clear indication of specific skills or responsibilities needed for the role. For example, some companies may use the title 'UX designer' to describe a role that involves both UX design and user research, while others may separate those roles into distinct titles (e.g. interaction designer and user researcher). You should focus on the skills and experience needed for the role and be open to different job titles that may encompass those skills. Leave the titles for later! Understanding these nuances can help you better navigate the job market and choose positions that better fit your circumstances. Breaking into the UX industry can be challenging, so I would advise you to be open to starting in entry-level positions to gain experience and build up your portfolio from there. Whenever I have a conversation about this topic with designers I'm mentoring, I always share with them these wise words from Sheryl Sandberg (former COO of Meta): '[Erik Schmidt] told me: "If you're offered a seat on a rocket ship, don't ask what seat! Just get on."'[6]

Keep getting out of your comfort zone

'Life begins at the end of your comfort zone' said author Neale Donald Walsch.[7] I wanted to end this chapter with these words because, for us designers, they can have an even deeper meaning. What I'm trying to say here is that, the more you progress in your career and the closer you get to your goals, the more you will encounter situations that will test both your skills and your perseverance. As humans, we are programmed to get comfortable once we achieve a certain amount of success. I'm advising you never to stay for too long in that comfort zone. Identify areas of your career that make you feel uncomfortable, and go there. Explore those areas, learn and accumulate knowledge. This can be anything from learning new skills, to taking on leadership roles to starting new ventures. This will keep your mind in the game, and it will make you a better and more experienced designer. Ultimately, it's an attitude that will make you stand out from the crowd.

In the end, what will matter the most in your new career is your love for design and your passion for bringing positive change to people's lives. I advise you to stay curious, keep learning and not be afraid to take risks. With a lot of persistence and hard work, you'll definitely find your starting place.

Notes

1   J Jarry. The Dunning-Kruger effect is probably not real, McGill, Office for Science and Society, 17 December 2020. www.mcgill.ca/oss/article/critical-thinking/dunning-kruger-effect-probably-not-real (archived at https://perma.cc/GW7L-7BPG)

2   L Buley (2013) *The User Experience Team of One: A research and design survival guide*, Rosenfeld Media, LLC, New York

3   M T Hansen. IDEO CEO Tim Brown: T-shaped stars: The backbone of IDEO's collaborative culture, Chief Executive Group, nd. chiefexecutive.net/ideo-ceo-tim-brown-t-shaped-stars-the-backbone-of-ideoaes-collaborative-culture__trashed (archived at https://perma.cc/H55L-JAHX)

4   K Vredenburg. Becoming a t-shaped designer, Karel Vredenburg, 20 July 2013. www.karelvredenburg.com/home/2013/7/20/becoming-a-t-shaped-designer (archived at https://perma.cc/2HY2-2SJB)

5   A Picchi (2022) *Design Management: Create, Develop, and Lead Effective Teams*, Apress, New York

6   S Sandberg (2015) *Lean In: Women, work, and the will to lead*, Penguin Random House, London

7   1440 Multiversity. 'Life begins at the end of your comfort zone': Talking with Neale Donald Walsch, 1440 Multiversity, 11 May 2019. www.1440.org/blog/life-begins-at-the-end-of-your-comfort-zone-talking-with-neale-donald-walsch (archived at https://perma.cc/9BX6-XSSM)

CHAPTER THIRTEEN

The interview

A h, the interview. You're almost there! This is the moment when all your hard work, preparation and dreams culminate in a single, hopefully awe-inspiring conversation with a potential employer. It's your chance to showcase your skills, experience and personality and leave a long-lasting impression that lands you your dream job as a UX designer. Or at least that's the theory. In practice, we all know that interviews can be daunting and, depending on your personality, it might be the hardest thing you've ever had to do. Your palms are sweating, your stomach feels like a swarm of angry bees, and your brain is telling you to leave the building immediately while at the same time trying to remember everything you've ever learned about UX. The first interview is enough to turn even the most confident of us into an emotional wreck.

But I have some good news for you. With the right preparation, it doesn't have to be like that. My goal in this chapter is to equip you with the proper knowledge and skills to navigate your job interview process confidently. I'll cover everything from what you need to do prior to applying to how to prepare for the interview all the way to questions you should expect to be asked during the interview. Finally, I'll go through some tips and tricks to help you turn that nervous energy into excitement and get your dream job as a UX designer.

Let's do this!

Portfolios

'Hey, what's going on here? I thought we were talking about the interview.' Well, without a portfolio, there aren't going to be an awful lot of interviews. Yes, that's right. Sorry to be so blunt about it. As an aspiring UX designer, if you don't have one, I can confidently say you won't even get an intro call. So, in a way, this *is* about the interview because to get there you need to start by building a portfolio.

A portfolio is a collection of your best design work. It should showcase your skills, experience and creativity, demonstrating your ability to solve complex problems and create great user experiences. You can look at it as tangible evidence of your accomplishments and skills. Remember that word 'evidence' because it will be important later. Having a strong portfolio is essential for getting selected for job interviews and ultimately landing those jobs and advancing your career. In this section of the book I'm going to teach you how to choose which type of portfolio is best for you, how to structure your work and how to present it in an interview successfully. My advice here is the result of having been on both sides of the table in probably hundreds of interviews.

Online or offline

But let's start by putting things into perspective. Largely there are two types of portfolios you can build: online (websites) and offline (files). Let's look at both of them and consider their advantages and disadvantages:

- *Online portfolios.* These are usually in the form of presentation websites, showing your work in an interactive way. The audience can choose which projects to view and what content to access at any time.
  - *Advantages:* Easy to access from any device. Highly interactive. Easy to share. Can host different types of content like videos or embedded apps. Can be used for both interviewing purposes and for creating a personal brand. You can always access the latest version live.
  - *Disadvantages:* Sometimes, online portfolios can be time-consuming to build and maintain. Some basic coding experience might be required.
- *Offline portfolios.* These are usually static presentations in various formats like PDF, PowerPoint, Keynote, etc.
  - *Advantages:* Easier to create and maintain.
  - *Disadvantages:* Difficult to share (they tend to be pretty significant in size) and, depending on the format you choose, do not necessarily work on all platforms or devices. Low interactivity (e.g. links and scrolling). You can only access the file that was shared.

My advice: start simple – design an offline portfolio first. I don't think I've ever heard about a designer with a good portfolio being rejected because they didn't have it live on a website. So, a static PDF file will get the job done. And that is a great starting point because you get to design it just the way you want, without having to worry too much about the front-end technology or bugs. Static portfolios are also highly preferred by recruiters because they can share them with their clients without giving away your identity.

In an ideal case, you should also have an online version of your portfolio, so if you can afford the luxury of time to build one, go for it. Some employers will appreciate the effort, and some nice and clever UX might make you stand out, but there are also some risks, like the website not working on a particular device or browser or the servers being painfully slow on the day of your interview. It happens all the time. Having both types of portfolios will give you the most flexibility when it comes to sharing them with recruiters or employers.

Format and content

Next, based on the structure and the type of content in your portfolio, I've seen two types: case studies; and UI-focused or gallery. Needless to say, I have a preference for the former because it gives the hiring manager a lot more context into your process, your skills and your personality. This type of portfolio format focuses on in-depth case studies that highlight your design process, the impact of your work and how you added value to the product. Case studies typically include a brief description of the initial situation, a problem statement, research findings, ideation samples and design solutions, and, finally, metrics or KPIs that demonstrate the success of the project. I would encourage you to put in the effort and structure your portfolio using case studies, because it will give you the highest chance of getting that dream job. I'm not even going to go too much into UI-focused portfolios because I don't think they tell the whole story, and they are just focused on a narrow niche. However, just for you to get a fair picture of what I'm talking about, they are those portfolios with eye-catching UI samples and little to no context on how the designer got there. Essentially, a gallery of (in most cases) good-looking user interfaces. For hiring managers these give very limited information of the skills of a designer and should be avoided, even if you are UI designer. Always try to describe the context and how your designs came to life.

Design

So, once you've decided which type of portfolio you're going to have, it's time to start designing it. Since you're a UX designer, why not follow a typical UX process for it? Do a bit of research, perhaps interview a few users (hiring managers in this case) and start sketching out some solutions. I'm not saying to reinvent the wheel, but depending on where you are, the market might have different demands when it comes to a portfolio. Don't just assume what they need. Ask a few of them! I've seen too many UX designers that fail to use UX best practices in their own portfolios.

From my experience there are a few important aspects to keep in mind while designing your portfolio. Since you already know who your 'users' are going to be, you need to design in it a way that it caters for their needs and goals. As a hiring manager myself, one of the biggest struggles I constantly face with regard to reviewing portfolios is *limited time*. Think about it from the hiring manager's perspective: sometimes they will get tens if not hundreds of applications, so in reality the person doing the hiring will not have time to go through your entire portfolio. What does this tell you? That you have to design it so that it immediately stands out from the crowd and communicates who you are as a UX designer in the shortest time possible. With that being said, I'll now share my top tips for designing your portfolio.

Quality over quantity

I'm starting with this one because, without it, everything else doesn't even matter. I can't stress this enough when speaking with aspiring designers about their portfolios. Please, and I do mean *please*, only include your best work. As designers, we often get excited and fall into the temptation of showing most, if not all, of our work in a portfolio because we want the hiring manager to see how hard working we are. Please don't do it! It will only have the inverse effect. Remember what I just said: hiring managers are time poor. The more information you include, the higher the chance they will miss vital information that you wish to get across. Imagine you are already fighting with the 'noise' of other people's CVs and portfolios. Don't also create noise in your own portfolio. My advice is to pick three of your best projects that show your end-to-end skills. That's it. Not eight, not six. Just three! And don't worry, if a hiring manager wants to see more of your work they will let you know. In terms of projects, make sure they show the different skills you have. For example, if one is more focused on the research and discovery part, the second should be more focused on user interface design, and so on. Show skills, diversity and clarity of process.

Always show your process

There is nothing I dislike more than seeing a portfolio that doesn't show any process. Including lots of screens and fancy visuals without any context doesn't help at all. As a hiring manager it makes me assume first you are not thinking about the user (me) and my needs, and second that since you're not showing it, maybe there is no process to show. Maybe you did go straight into designing the interface. What I want to see is your design process, so include artefacts from research, ideation, prototyping and testing. Explain how you ended up with certain design decisions and how they contributed to the success of the product. *Always. Show. Process!*

Tell a story

As I mentioned before, I wholeheartedly recommend using the case study format for your portfolio. But don't just make it a dry sequence of events starting from research and ending up with screens of the final designs. Design the case study like a story. You need to immerse your hiring manager in that story. I usually tell the designers I'm mentoring that a case study needs to be very similar to a comic book. You need to create a setting, you need to show an intriguing situation and take the user through all this journey until you reach a conclusion. Be strategic about how you show your work. Remember, choosing only three items in your portfolio allows you to spend more time on the things that really matter, like how you deliver the information. My advice is to use the basics of storytelling for this. Use a narrative arc approach to present your case study. At high level, you should split your case study story into multiple stages (Figure 13.1):

1   *Exposition:* The background of the 'story'. Tell the user about the setting, the goals, the team, the vision behind your product and the role you play in all this.
2   *Initial conflict:* This is the key starting point of the case study. The 'why' behind it. Why are you embarking on this journey? With what goals?
3   *Rising action:* Describe events that add suspense. For example, a stakeholder might have disagreed, or the research pointed to a completely different problem.
4   *Climax:* The most important part of the story. This is your opportunity to shine. What did you do to turn things around? What was the value you brought to the project?
5   *Falling action:* Describe how the story developed after your intervention. What did the team do, what did you change and how?
6   *Resolution:* Probably a good point in time to bring in some metrics or KPIs. How did your work impact the product? What had changed compared to before?
7   *Denouement:* Final conclusion and considerations. Your chance to shine again. Highlight how you were instrumental to the whole thing.

FIGURE 13.1 The stages of a narrative arc

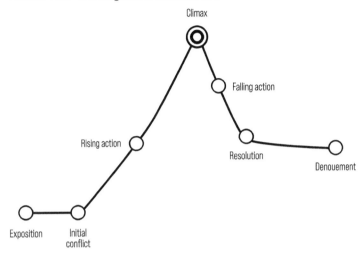

By structuring your case study as a story, you keep the hiring manager focused and they are likely to dedicate more time to reviewing your work. Naturally this increases your chances of making it to the interview and getting the job.

Language matters

This is very related to the above. It's not enough to structure your case study like a story. You also need to adjust your language and delivery according to the purpose of a portfolio. Again, let's recap. What is the purpose of a portfolio, in a nutshell? A portfolio is not an art gallery and definitely not a collection of snapshots from your project. A portfolio's main purpose is to get you to the interview and get you hired. Crafting a portfolio is an effort in effectively highlighting your abilities and using your marketing expertise. Remember what we discussed in Chapter 9 about mastering communications, and apply all that learning here. Try to use clear and concise language to explain your thinking process, solutions and impact. Avoid using excessive jargon or technical terms that may be difficult for non-designers to understand (not all hiring managers will have a design background). Use bullet points, clear headings and visual elements to make your portfolio easy to scan and navigate. Last but not least – don't use too much text. Remember, your users don't have much time. Try to deliver your message as concisely as possible.

Show attention to detail

When reviewing designer portfolios, the ones that stand out the most to me are those where I can clearly see that the person has spent time, effort and thought on every little detail. That's because when hiring for a designer, attention to detail matters – it's a measure of your skills and your love for the craft. This can be the difference between a successful job application and a portfolio that gets discarded. So make sure you spend enough time on things like layout, typography, imagery, etc. Also – watch out for spelling errors. There's nothing more annoying than a portfolio full of typos.

Hopefully this advice will help you craft the best portfolio possible. But once the hiring manager decides you could be right for the job, in comes the next part – the interview.

'UX designing' your interview

So here we are, the final step – the interview. You've created an amazing portfolio, gone through your intro call with flying colours and now it's time to face the hiring managers. As I mentioned before, this process can be nerve-racking, so my main goal here is to teach you how to go through this stage confidently and reach your objective.

I've named this section 'UX designing' your interview because this is what we're going to do. We're going to look at the 'user' needs and design their experience based on that. So what do hiring managers need from you at this stage? Good news! Since you're already at the interview stage, they must have liked both your CV and portfolio and are considering you for the job. In a sense, half of the battle is already won, so good job! Next, it all comes down to reassurance. That's it! This is what the interview (or interviews if you have multiple stages) is all about. In order to make a good impression and get the job you need to remove all fears or doubts from the interviewer's mind. So how can you do that? As you can imagine, it all comes down to preparation.

First and foremost, make sure you do in-depth research about the company and everything surrounding the role. Try to get familiar with the industry they are operating in, the products they have and the company's mission and values. These will be important in the entire interview process, because someone who does not do their basic research looks uninterested in the role, and that is a sure way to lose their trust. Check out their websites, apps and social media profiles and try to get a sense of who they are. It's also a good idea to research the company through the lens of the people who work or used to work there, so checking out sites like Glassdoor or LinkedIn should give you more insights into what the work culture there is like. The same goes for the job description. Make sure you study it, because it will help answer some of your doubts and also provide you with an opportunity to ask your own questions based on its content. By doing this, you avoid asking questions that are already answered in the job description, which could make you look like you are not paying attention to details.

If you spend too much time practising for the interview by talking to yourself in the mirror you might start to sound less natural, and more robotic and insecure. However, many of you out there will be introverts (I know I am one) so it's very important to take the time to think about what you want to say in the interview and make sure you provide clear answers that convey your message. One technique I would recommend for this is *writing down your thoughts* before the interview. Yes, as simple as that. I recommend doing this on the same day as the interview. Set and hour or so aside and write down the important things, like how you plan to introduce yourself and talk about your process, your motivation and goals, and so on. Mark Murphy explains why this approach is effective:

> Encoding is the biological process by which the things we perceive travel to our brain's hippocampus where they're analyzed. From there, decisions are made about what gets stored in our long-term memory and, in turn, what gets discarded. Writing improves that encoding process. In other words, when you write it down it has a much greater chance of being remembered.[1]

This technique will help you put your thoughts in order, reduce anxiety and enable you to answer interview questions in a much more natural way that will not sound rehearsed. With time, you will get very good at this, and if you're like me you will use this technique before any important presentation or meeting.

So, you made to it to the actual interview, your portfolio is ready and you feel prepared for the interviewers questions. Remember what I mentioned before about *creating reassurance*. This should be your main goal in the interview. There are small differences between a remote and an on-site interview but largely your goals should look the same: making them feel comfortable and confident about choosing you for the role. Remember, especially for on-site interviews, the actual interview starts before you get to a meeting room. Because they don't know you yet, people will naturally try to assess your behaviour, personality and professionalism based on how you act outside the interview. Make sure that you politely greet everyone, maintain eye contact throughout the conversation, and smile and enjoy the moment.

During the interview is when you need to really shine. What I'm going to tell you next might seem a bit counterintuitive, but hear me out. If you want to do really well in the interview, pace yourself a bit. Try to strike a balance between managing the anxiety of meeting new people and the excitement of talking about UX, your experience and your portfolio. You need be calm and composed, while *at the same time* conveying your enthusiasm for UX. Let me teach you a trick that will help. Hopefully, you applied for the job because UX design is your passion. Use that to your advantage. Speaking passionately about a subject you love is an anxiety killer. Don't be afraid to show your true self, even if sometimes that might mean revealing some of you vulnerabilities. People will appreciate you for your self-awareness.

Next, I want to go through some suggestions that will be useful to you during the actual interview:

- *Learn to listen to your interviewer.* As a UX designer I'm sure you're already good at listening, but I wanted to remind you anyway. Don't rush in – take the time to understand their questions fully before answering. This will help you provide more thoughtful and relevant answers. Also, a bit of a no-brainer, but don't interrupt your interviewer when they're speaking.

- *Respond to questions in a clear and concise manner.* Try to limit your answers to 30 seconds to one minute. Usually, if it takes longer than that to respond you are going into too much detail. Use simple and clear language, and avoid using too much technical jargon as your interviewer might not be familiar with all of it.

- *Avoid going off at a tangent.* This one happens very often in interviews, when the candidate tries to answer an interviewer's question but ends up contemplating a completely new subject. This can be very damaging to your credibility, as you will come across as unstructured or disorganized. Whenever you're giving details about a topic, ask yourself if those details are actually relevant to the conversation.

- *Tell the story.* Because you've used storytelling techniques to structure your portfolio (remember what we learned in the previous section), this should come easily to you now. Follow the narrative thread and take advantage of having this in place. Give the interviewers time for questions and go into details if you feel there is value. Explain the problem you were trying to solve, the design process you used and the impact of your work. In the end, don't forget to highlight the results of your work, showing how the metrics improved.

- *Don't 'read the teleprompter'.* This applies to interviews or any other setting where you need to present something from a screen. Your audience can read as well, so don't just read them the text you see on screen. Focus on the story and use natural language to lead the interviewer through your 'story'. This will make you feel more comfortable and you will come across as confident and inspiring.

- *Do not be overly critical of other people's UX work.* In many interviews you might be asked to critique an app or a design that was created by someone else. This can be a delicate moment and you need to handle it gracefully. Try to be empathetic about it. First and foremost, you don't have any information about the context that design was created in. You might be unaware of technical limitations, budget constraints or product goals. A good UX designer would critique the work in a professional manner, in a respectful way, and mention the lack of context as an important factor. This will show you are realistic and grounded.

- *Don't be afraid to ask questions.* Remember, interviews works both ways. In some ways you are also interviewing the hiring manager and the company. Don't be afraid to ask questions about the company or the position. This will show them that you're engaged and interested in the job. But also don't overdo it, don't bombard the interviewer with too many irrelevant question. A good balance would be for 90 per cent of the questions to come from the interviewer and 10 per cent from you.

- *Don't oversell yourself or your skills.* Again, a delicate one, as it can be pretty subjective depending on who's interviewing you. Try to strike a balance between being very confident in promoting yourself and being aware of the areas where you still need to improve.

And finally, here are a couple things you *should not* be doing in an UX interview because they might cost you the job:

- *Being arrogant.* Avoid coming across as arrogant or dismissive of the interviewer's questions or feedback in relation to your portfolio. Show humility and a willingness to learn. It's ok to show confidence, but make sure it's balanced with a realistic view of yourself.
- *Getting defensive.* As designers, we sometimes get defensive when we are given negative feedback on our work. This is a pretty normal reaction, especially for designers just starting out in the field. If the interviewer asks you a challenging question, try to listen and respond thoughtfully. They are not doing this to put you down. They might offer genuinely valuable feedback, so make sure you take everything onboard gracefully.

Hopefully, using my advice here you will be able to make a good impression in your interview and showcase your amazing talent and personality. Go and get that dream job! You can do this!

Note

1 M Murphy. Neuroscience explains why you need to write down your goals if you actually want to achieve them, Forbes, 15 April 2018, www.forbes.com/sites/markmurphy/2018/04/15/neuroscience-explains-why-you-need-to-write-down-your-goals-if-you-actually-want-to-achieve-them (archived at https://perma.cc/YMJ3-KNVB)

CHAPTER FOURTEEN

Designing your future career

You've finally made it. You've got your first UX designer job, and you couldn't be more thrilled about it. But your work doesn't stop here. 'Designing' your future career can be essential for both your professional growth and your personal development. As an aspiring UX designer, you've made yourself familiar with the industry and gained your first real-world experience in the field. But what's next? How and when should you take your career to the next level to achieve your goals?

In this chapter I focus on giving advice to UX designers who are looking to advance their careers. We'll explore various career paths and progression opportunities available to UX designers, and I'll provide practical guidance on how to navigate the industry in the best possible way. Finally, we're going to wrap up by looking at the day-to-day life of a UX designer through an amusing lens.

Career paths and progression

UX design is a career with many exciting paths and opportunities. Whether you're just starting out as a junior designer or are an industry veteran, there is an abundance of ways to progress your career. In this section, we'll look at potential career paths, some best practices and things to avoid if you want to be on track for success.

In general, your career progression within UX design can depend on multiple aspects, such as your skills, your personality type, the type of career track you want to pursue, the size of your team and your long-term goals.

Let's start with my favourite one: the career track. Historically, there was one single career track that ran from junior positions all the way to senior, manager and then leadership. Everything was clear, and people knew what they needed to do to progress. Except it was all wrong! This resulted in many good professionals becoming managers without having the required people skills, just because they wanted to progress in their careers and avoid hitting the proverbial glass ceiling. However, as one insightful commentator has said, 'Many people in our industry are introverts. They excel in using their hard skills in solitude. They have fewer people skills than others in the workplace. This makes it harder for them to rise above others who have better soft skills.'[1]

Organizations have now realized this was not the right approach, and many have adopted a dual-track strategy offering two potential career tracks: individual contributor (IC); and manager/leader. These two essentially progress in the same way up to the senior level. From there on, professionals with good people skills might choose to become managers, while highly skilled people that do not want to manage a team can still progress successfully in their careers.

In the UX field, once you hit the senior level, it's time to start thinking about what your next steps are. Some people decide to remain ICs, while others pursue management or leadership roles. In reality, many companies still don't offer the IC role, while others that do and promise to offer a similar progression to the management track don't really enable that in practice. The truth is that IC roles, in the majority of cases, will hit that invisible glass ceiling at some point. So, if you ever want to find yourself in a leadership role, chances are that you will be forced to take the management route.

I should also stress that the more you advance in your career, the less hands-on you will be. For those of you who cannot see yourself parting with your research, wireframing or prototyping, it's likely that the management route is not for you. I've met designers who made the conscious choice to go into management only to go back to being ICs in a matter of months because they were missing the craft. Management is not for everyone!

Next, let's take skills as an element in your career progression. Although most UX designers will choose to be generalists because they enjoy more the end-to-end process or want access to more job opportunities, others will want to specialize in certain areas of UX. Remember the T-shaped or M-shaped professional? At a high level, there are four main specializations you can pursue in UX:

- *User researchers:* More focused on the research, usability testing and analysis of user needs.
- *Interaction designers:* More focused on designing, prototyping and testing user interfaces.
- *UI designers:* Only focused on the visual part of interaction design and on creating design systems.
- *UX writers:* A more niche role focused on creating the content strategy and micro-copy of a product.

I now have a few critical pieces of advice I would like to share with you that might help you boost your career progression speed. These are things to do or not to do in your career. Keep in mind that these might not apply to every one of you, because of your individual circumstances, but give them a read nonetheless:

- *Don't stay in one job forever.* I know this advice goes against what many career advisers would tell you. You're going to hear a lot about continuity and loyalty and how employers tend to favour those who don't change jobs very often: 'Tenure at a job is vital for appealing to future employers – that's the prevailing narrative in the workforce, even though many workers frequently change jobs and have for years.'[2] However, I want to challenge this philosophy from two points of view. First, when push comes to shove, big organizations will proceed to do massive layoffs if it best suits their financial interests. Now, where's the loyalty in that? Second, staying in a job for too long can be detrimental to both your skills and your personal finances. Both can lag behind the market if you don't move from time to time. It's statistically proven that the chance of increasing your salary is higher when you change jobs compared to getting salary increases in the same role. An article in Forbes clearly spells it out: 'Employees who stay in companies longer than two years get paid 50% less'.[3] I'm not saying you shouldn't be loyal to your company, I'm just saying you need to treat this as a healthy business relationship and prioritize yourself.
- *Work on personal projects.* I give this advice to every designer I mentor. Having a project outside your main job can give you new perspectives and will keep your creative juices flowing. Because there will be less pressure to deliver, you can practise at your own pace. By projects, I mean anything from designing your own app to starting a community or interviewing interesting people.
- *Think business. This is not optional.* During my career, I've met so many designers that don't give any thought to the actual needs of the business. They declare themselves as user advocates and completely detach themselves from reality on

the ground. Needless to say, this never ends well, generating misalignment and tensions in the product team. I love what Jhilmil Jain (Director of Product at Google) said on this topic:

To set yourself up for a successful UX career, you need to shift your mindset from that of a product designer to a product owner by embracing the business side of design. While it's difficult to change your thinking habits, it goes a long way in making you more effective – both with your immediate team and in the partnerships you need to forge to turn your ideas into fully realized products.[4]

- *Leave your ego at the door.* Be *really* open to feedback. This is particularly noticeable with designers that are in their first years of practising UX. The inability to genuinely accept feedback hinders your career progression and creates unwanted anxiety in your work life. This aspect will not resolve by itself, so you will need to work on it tirelessly to educate yourself out of this bad habit. The first step is realizing you have a problem. José Torre comments on this very topic:

The attachment dilemma:
Many designers tend to be very defensive when it comes to their work, I guess it's just in our nature. A big majority comes from an artistic background, which makes us see the things that we make as an extension of ourselves, they're our little babies. This puts us in a defensive position every time someone says something that challenges what we made. Essentially, if you say something bad about my work, it's like you're saying that about me.

The explosive combination:
When these two things combine, you end up with designers who are 'drunk' on praise and are unable to detach themselves from their creations. This combination is really explosive and the reason why many designers can't take a critique without responding with a counter-attack.[5]

- *Don't be afraid to experiment.* There will come a time in your career when you'll feel equipped with the necessary tools to question well-established UX norms or best practices. At first, you will feel nervous about this, many times because of peer pressure ('That's not the way we've been doing it' attitude) or self-doubt. I want to remind you that design as a field was built on experimentation. This is how it evolved over time. This is why this field is different from so many others. You don't even need to ask permission to do it. Have an idea for a new methodology? Try it! What's the worst that can happen?
- *You are a lens, embrace it.* Finally, as UX designers, we are taught that user needs are at the core of what we do and we should follow this practice religiously. But in reality, every bit of information that you gather, every user need, every business goal or technical limitation will pass through one lens: *you.* It's time to embrace this and 'Instead of just skills, focus on your lens – the unique way you see the world and the types of questions that excite you. Your lens reaches laterally, transcending any one discipline, job description, or skillset. It's the worldview that threads your varied interests.'[6]

As you've learned in this part of the book, there are many choices available when it comes to your career progression in UX. No matter which path you choose, the most important advice I can give you is to keep learning and keep investing in yourself.

A day in the life of a UX designer

It seems suitable to end this book on a positive note, so in this section let's take a moment to reflect on the things you've learned and the incredible impact you can have on our world as a UX designer. We've explored the ins and outs of user experience design, including its importance, process and key methods. We've discussed the foundations of UX, interaction design and evaluating user experience, and you've discovered how UX strategy can help you get your ideas across successfully. Finally, we've looked into some guidance for those of you interested in pursuing a career in UX. But all of this can be meaningless without one thing: the passion to improve other people's lives. When we think about UX, it's easy to get lost in the technical details – the wireframes, the prototypes, or analysing user research data. But, as you've learned in this book, at its core, UX design is about people. It's about understanding their needs, frustrations and desires, and creating products that make their lives better. When we intentionally design for people, we have the power to create experiences that are truly meaningful, experiences that go way beyond a successful product and that touch people's lives in a deep way. As a UX designer, you have the power to shape the way people interact with technology and, by extension, the way they interact with each other. You will be able to generate emotions, build trust, improve people's quality of life and overall, have the chance to contribute to a better world. I would say you have the responsibility to use your skills and knowledge to make people's lives better. When we design with empathy in mind, the possibilities are endless.

But with great power comes great responsibility. The field of UX is constantly evolving, and it can be easy to get caught up in the latest trends and buzzwords. It's important to always remember why you're doing this. It's about listening to people's needs, empathizing with their struggles, and creating solutions that truly make a difference in their lives. Remember these words.

So, to all you aspiring UX designers out there, remember why you got into this field in the first place. Was it to create beautiful interfaces? Or to solve complex problems? Or was it to make a real difference to people's lives? Whatever your motivation, never lose sight of the fact that your work has the power to touch the lives of millions of people around the world.

As you embark on your UX journey, remember to stay empathetic and remain true to your values. Don't be afraid to break the rules sometimes. Learn from your failures, celebrate your successes, and always remember that the most important aspect of UX design is the people.

To continue developing your UX skills and knowledge, it's essential to stay curious, ask questions and always be willing to learn and try new things. Keep up with industry trends, attend conferences and network with other UX professionals. Also, remember to get yourself mentors – they will boost your career in ways you can never imagine. And again, most importantly, don't be afraid to fail. Iteration is a crucial part of UX and that is true for your career as well. We learn best from our mistakes.

If you're like me, being a UX designer is not just a job. It's a calling. A calling to put empathy at the forefront of your work and to never lose sight of the fact that you have the power to shape the future of technology and the world around you. So, to all future UX designers out there, I want to thank you for your passion, your creativity and your commitment to creating a better world. Your work matters and I can't wait to see what amazing things you will create in the years to come.

UX design is a fascinating and rewarding field. I hope this book has inspired you to continue exploring it. See you on the other side.

Notes

1 G Maguire, Effective Managers Must Have People Skills, ESRI Arcuser, Summer 2017, www.esri.com/about/newsroom/arcuser/effective-managers-must-have-people-skills (archived at https://perma.cc/FF8N-LP7X)

2 K Morgan. Some workers stay put at a single company for several years – even decades. Is this a signal of loyalty or laziness? BBC, 10 August 2022. www.bbc.com/worklife/article/20220808-can-you-stay-in-a-job-for-too-long (archived at https://perma.cc/MLY4-QHAE)

3 C Keng. Employees who stay in companies longer than two years get paid 50% less, Forbes, 22 June 2014. www.forbes.com/sites/cameronkeng/2014/06/22/employees-that-stay-in-companies-longer-than-2-years-get-paid-50-less (archived at https://perma.cc/2UCE-AZAY)

4 J Jain. How to have a successful UX career at Google (or anywhere else), Medium, 1 November 2019. medium.com/google-design/how-to-have-a-successful-ux-career-at-google-or-anywhere-else-ea63624f74de (archived at https://perma.cc/6DFX-A6SM)

5 J Torre. Hey designer, why so fragile? Medium, 31 July 2017. uxdesign.cc/hey-designer-why-so-fragile-57e7292c0a51 (archived at https://perma.cc/G6FB-DBJU)

6 P Talwai. Finding a voice as a non-traditional UX researcher, Medium, 4 June 2019. medium.com/google-design/finding-a-voice-as-a-non-traditional-ux-researcher-d58e66c3f80b (archived at https://perma.cc/A3UQ-2XEX)

Index